From

Marginal

to

Magnificent

How to Make Your Marriage Sing

STEPHEN W. FRUEH, PHD

Published by Advantage, Charleston, South Carolina.
Member of Advantage Media Group.

ADVANTAGE is a registered trademark and the Advantage colophon is a trademark of Advantage Media Group, Inc.

Printed in the United States of America.

ISBN: 978-1-59932-142-4
LCCN: 2009936321

This publication is designed to provide accurate and authoritative information in regard to the subject matter covered. It is sold with the understanding that the publisher is not engaged in rendering legal, accounting, or other professional services. If legal advice or other expert assistance is required, the services of a competent professional person should be sought.

Most Advantage Media Group titles are available at special quantity discounts for bulk purchases for sales promotions, premiums, fundraising, and educational use. Special versions or book excerpts can also be created to fit specific needs.

For more information, please write: Special Markets, Advantage Media Group, P.O. Box 272, Charleston, SC 29402 or call 1.866.775.1696.

Visit us online at **advantagefamily**.com

Acknowledgements

I acknowledge the great gifts of patience, love, forgiveness and time numerous friends have given. I acknowledge the many couples who trusted me with their marriage and many friends who read the manuscript and offered helpful suggestions though I take complete responsibility for this work and its evolution.

Here's a short list of thanks. Paul Fairweather, friend and mentor, who believed me. Dan Rothstein, wise counselor, challenger and inspiration. Robert Bly, who carries a deep sense of masculine loving to those he mentors, Michael Meade who turned his ear to me and James Hillman for all he wrote and writes.

I thank my Swiss father for life, my two older brothers, Otto and Wes, for their loving guidance, patience and continuity, my sister Esther for always loving and my four foot ten inch Swedish mother for her melancholy and her stories.

There are men and women who would have no idea that I would thank them. I thank them now for their rejection, seduction, control, manipulation, invasion, dismissal, shame and more. For it is those who forged in me a resiliency and determination to descend into what is true of me and thereby find a pathway to legitimacy.

And I thank with huge tears of gratitude George DuVall, the Pennsylvania farmer who took me in at thirteen and a half and introduced me to the beauty of being a man.

I acknowledge, thank and bless my life partner who knows how to say no, my wife Lynn. She says no so firmly that her yes, often barely audible, stirs my soul. And I thank my children – all and each of them – for their soul stirring love and profound loyalty.

Though I never did read the book, I thank Teri Cole Whitaker for her title – *What You Think of Me Is Absolutely None of My Business* and at the center of everything I thank my heavenly Father and Mother Earth for their sustenance.

Much thanks to Dan Grant of www.idigdesign.com for his creation of graphics in the text; huge thanks to Amy Ropp of Advantage Media Group for her patience, good will and encouragement, and Ellie Davis who is a force to be reckoned with. She gave big doses of 'tough love' editing. What we missed is mine, what works, hers. The cover art is by Xenos Mesa, a man of incredible talent.

Stephen W. Frueh M.Div., Ph.D.

The Miracle in This

Nine months before any of us arrived –
the moments before even that –
the faucet may have been dripping,
a persistent weed might have poked up through the tomatoes,
she may have implored, he may have said yes –
What conversation was the accompaniment to our conception
as we spotted our chance to shoot through to this place?

> ...and us – all of us – any of us: lovers now,
> having found each other the day our paths crossed,
> each able to say simply yes - "I knew I loved him
> from the moment I first saw him..."
> Or "Nothing seemed different"..."I just asked her how she cooked
> artichokes..."
> Or "...it was a day like any other day..."

It's easy to look back and see how our steps converge to meet
at the altar of miracles, God saying "I now pronounce you:
lover, partner, biker, writer, mother of Zuri (heart exploding with so much joy), father"
aiming us at the congregation,
pushing us out to "Go forth this way."
Whoever knows
what these yeses set in motion...
what is shifted mightily by their whisper,
and so: becomes seen, that which might so easily have been overlooked;
becomes what so easily: Might Not Have Been.
Like a dark hall changed by the opening of a door
to one brightly lit room.
There: other doors!
A magnificent portrait on the wall!
A brilliant woven carpet on which we walk!

Lynn Comley Frueh (reprinted with permission)

Preface

Marriage offers an agreement a profound commitment for people who wish to create a micro-community that they can call home. It is an agreement which 'holds them' in commitment to shared values and ideals over time. Marriage is born of overwhelmingly positive feelings. We can safely say every couple begins marriage with the intention of it lasting a lifetime. We rejoice at partnering with someone who feels like a natural friend, an interesting lover, a companion and a potential partner for life.

Most couples do not define what they mean by "marriage." Instead, they assume they each mean the same thing when they say: "I do." To discover that they really didn't know what they meant, or intended, or promised when they married, can be very painful. Worse, the discovery that they had no idea what their partner meant when they spoke those two small words can be devastating.

Divorce, though not our focus here, hovers around 50%. Our focus is the 60-70% of marriages that are arguably the pipeline of divorce where couples live a marginally satisfying life together.

We offer a 'cure' for marginal marriages. If both partners will commit to looking at what is marginalized in their marriage, if they'll commit to taking individual responsibility for cleaning out the debris that has piled up between them over the years, if they'll examine and, perhaps, reinvent the paradigm upon which their idea of marriage is based – their marriage, your marriage, will create a new lease on life. Marriage, we believe, offers a continual opportunity for rebirth. This is the premise of my work and the foundation of this book.

After years of studying our own marriage I have designed a new model – a fresh approach to the marriage conversation (in our marriage I am the model builder, Lynn, my partner, is the 'reality principle' or truth tester). We intend to fully challenge you to maximize the potential of your partnership. We hope this book helps you do that. We hope it helps your marriage sing.

Stephen W. Frueh M.Div., Ph.D., April 15, 2009

Until One Is Committed

Until one is committed there is hesitancy. There is the chance to draw back, which always leads to ineffectiveness. Concerning all acts of initiative and creation there is one elementary truth, the ignorance of which kills countless ideas and splendid plans: The moment one definitely commits oneself, Providence moves too. All sorts of things have a tendency to occur that help what would never otherwise have transpired. A whole stream of events issues from the decision, raising in one's favor all manner of unforeseen incidents and meetings and material assistance, which no man could have dreamed would come his way.

"Whatever you can do, or dream you can, begin it. Boldness has genius, power and magic in it." –GOETHE

"Believe nothing, no matter where you read it or who has said it, not even if I have said it, unless it agrees with your own reason and your own common sense." –BUDDHA

Table of Contents

How to Read this book

This book isn't meant to be read cover to cover like you would a novel. Most self-help books aren't. When you try to read a self-help book all the way through, you're apt to get discouraged. Which is why a whole lot of people have a whole lot of books with markers sticking out about a third of the way in.

A good book on relationships will include the basic categories most of us are interested in – healthy sexuality, money, listening/communicating, conflict, visioning and so on.

Advice, exercises, explanations and theories on any of these subjects can be really helpful, but you don't eat a gourmet meal the way you wash down a burger at Mac's lounge. With a special meal, you take it one bite at a time. And, you don't have to be good, as Mary Oliver reminds us in her stunningly beautiful poem "Wild Geese." "You do not have to be good. You do not have to walk on your knees /for a hundred miles through the desert, repenting…"

So, read the introductions (I have a habit of continually writing new ones so there may be two or three by time I truck this over to the publisher) – then read the first few paragraphs of a section that interests you today, right now, when thinking about your relationship. Then, put whatever you get from that into practice right away. Right away. Don't wait to talk it over. Act on it.

Relationships sing if you don't spend a lot of time mucking around "considering" stuff. "Gee, that's interesting" and so on. When you see something you'd like to act on, do it immediately. In this way, you'll quickly begin moving your marriage into a new and vital exchange of ideas.

One more thing. Actually two. A good friend of mine, Dr. Bruce Derman, has written a good book for couples with this title: *We'd Have a Great Relationship if it Weren't For You.* I sell a lot of them to clients of mine. Here's what I tell them.

"Buy this book. You don't have to read it. Buy it. Put it on your coffee table or kitchen counter. Look at the title everyday. Remind yourself of this simple principle: Everything that's right and good that's going to happen in this relationship is 100% up to me. And, I have faith that my partner says the same thing to herself about herself." Take full responsibility for the quality of your marriage. Act on it now.

Oh, and the other thing? Go ahead and read it anyway. It's a good book. And, you don't have to read it in one sitting.

Introduction

"We must dance and we must sing for we are blessed by everything and everything we see is blessed." —WILLIAM BUTLER YEATS

The Wow! of Marriage

Introducing you to the ever-alert inner-dynamo that you've so carefully suppressed, shamed, ignored and brutalized over the course of most of your adult life takes focus and courage. Can it be that the *you* within you is not yet fully revealed to you?

This book is for people who are sick of ordinary, repetitive conversations that produce numbingly predictable outcomes. "How'd your day go?" and "What's going on?" are the usual beginners in these conversations.

Some of us are like the mowing machines I operated on the farm as a teenaged hired hand. They cut the alfalfa indiscriminate of the individual character of each blade of grass and its individual uniqueness. The mower's goal was speed and efficiency.

Marriage conversations descend into efficiency because we haven't had a better idea for a long, long time. Efficiency, you may have noticed, breeds contempt.

To let go of efficiency and embrace healthy dialogue, try a little archeological experiment. Take a hard look at your life. There is an astounding group of stories within. Just think: a very long time ago you learned to walk. To walk! There were no books, no courses, not even a very competent model available on how to walk. Yet you stood, wobbled, risked, fell and stood again. Soon you were walking, then running then running and jumping. In time your competency in walking was taken totally for granted.

Somewhere somehow during this incredible accomplishment you were working on another unbelievably complicated competency. That's right – you were learning language. Learning to understand what others were saying to you and learning to form your own words and sentences.

All this learning took place in the first five years of your life. Consider the stories you would tell if you could remember what it was like for you to learn to walk and talk.

Later on you fell in love. You probably never learned to fall in love but you did it anyway. And most of us never received any intentional instruction on how to take that love and make it into something solid, long lasting and beautiful. We believed that if we were really "in love" everything would work out fine. Think of the stories lying dormant in your psyche around your experiments with love.

I can tell you this. I'm in love with writing – have several filing cabinets full of stuff I've written over the years. That love, however, doesn't translate into great writing. I'm still on a steep learning curve, still reading everything I can, still listening to mentors and still waiting for the first great book to roll out of my computer.

The stories within us point to numerous adventures, journeys and unspeakable obstacles to our coming into our own. *Here's a secret.* Your partner, too, has stories you've never heard. Stories of immense courage, touching spiritual depth, profound vulnerability and resolute determination.

Why haven't you heard these stories? And why are your own stories still buried within the detritus of your life?

To cure "What's up?" and "Honey I'm home," you'll have to begin digging out the uniqueness that you bring to this world. You'll have to partner in this archeological adventure because stories take a teller and a listener. Stories come alive when an interested other is giving their full attention to the drama unfolding. Stories light up with the involvement of others. To prove this, all you have to do is tell a story to an average four or five year old child. Their enthusiasm creates your enthusiasm. Watch the story fill out, become emotional, extend beyond the mere facts. Watch it because it's as close to magic as you'll get. This book is about bringing singing and dancing and stories and intimate conversation back into your marriage. Your life is a collection of songs – some blues, some rock, some classical, some hymns. We invite you to open to the library of music within and start bringing it to the kitchen table.

We'll be waiting to hear your song.

I. Marginal to Magnificent

A. What's Possible?

When my daughter, then seven, made lemonade to sell at a small makeshift stand in front of our home, she asked me to buy more cups. I said, "Honey, you have plenty of cups, at least 30 or so. Our street doesn't get much traffic." She looked at me as if I just told her it was snowing. Then she said, "But daddy, I don't want to run out!"

She has big visions. She's not afraid to dream. She's almost always on the side of the best possible outcome, and she knows how to "stay in leadership." My daughter doesn't easily yield her dreams to the fears of others.

My daughter expects a lot out of life. Many people expect little. This is especially true of marriage where it's easy to dumb down expectations. Easy to settle. Easy to complain about our partners and not examine what it is that we bring to the table.

I know a couple who describe their marriage like this: "It ain't bad. It ain't good. I suppose it's all you can expect after 23 years together." Another couple told me recently that, "We don't fight and I suppose that's good. But we don't talk much, about anything important anyway, so I suppose that's not so good."

Some of us settle for boredom. Some of us grow cynical. A lot of us think that if we're "getting along ok" that that's good enough. There are couples who have a "Hi honey, I'm home. What's on TV?" relationship. There are couples who argue continuously and couples who never argue at all. All of these qualify as missing the immense potential within marriage.

Since many of us can more easily see a speck in our partner's eye than the storm clouds in our own, we tend toward diagnosis and analysis of our partners rather that productively creating new pathways to intimacy.

Psychotherapy has focused on relationship competencies as a kind of cure for dysfunction. That's not surprising because psychotherapists want to help couples with the problems they present. That's good because we all need to be more competent problem solvers, but there's a more foundational challenge.

We have discovered within many couples a deep longing to realize a promise they felt long ago, a promise buried by years of neglect, disappointments, relational incompetency and lack of information.

That promise has lacked a muscular paradigm, a model that could and would support the generation of an expansive attitude towards marriage. Commitment to a real partnership, a paradigm or "model of reality" that lends a context to your aspirations is fundamental to changing the quality of your life.

Marriage shapes our expectations for loving. It holds us by the definition we give it to a life of earnest work and realization of the natural consequences of loving, of nesting and of community.

From *Marginal to Magnificent* is about this: the model of marriage we have lived with is not clear to most of us, it's not compelling and it's out of date.

Our model of marriage is a cobbled together one – part 12th century romantic idealism, part 15th century pragmatics, the protection of property, which included women, children and cattle, and part 20th century grand party wedding. When is the last time you went to a wedding and found it interesting?

We asked, in *With These Rings*, what would it take to create a model of marriage that could carry us over the years, that would compel us to continually explore our individual possibilities, the capacity to love and uncover in ever deeper layers the reasons we partnered in the first place?

What would it take to create a model in which we could sing its praises, enjoy its challenges, affirm our own loving and celebrate our families – our micro communities – in the context of the larger communities in which we live? What would it take to enjoy an ecologically sound, philosophically defensible, generative center of healthy relationships that could provide the foundations of creativity and sanctuary for future generations?

My daughter's lemonade stand, already grounded in its viability, would need quality lemonade, plenty of cups and an increase in traffic on our street. Beyond that, however, it would need her passion and belief that her lemonade was the best in the world.

For us it might look like this:

B. Three Things to Consider in Creating Your Own Model of Marriage

1. Music Theory: The Fundamentals of Song in Marriage

You'll need a clear and compelling philosophy of marriage. A philosophy is a belief and value structure that informs our decisions and actions, even our attitudes, in good and not so good times. To enjoy your marriage song you'll want to bring your own philosophy of marriage back onto center stage.

What this means is I'm inviting you to say out loud what you mean by marriage. Don't be afraid to do this. You are walking around with assumptions about marriage – what it 'should' look like, how your partner 'should' show up, what you 'should' be able to expect if your marriage were healthy. These 'shoulds' equal your not yet fully articulated philosophy of marriage. There's work to be done here. Get started and your relationship will start to change.

Have you asked anyone lately, married for more than a month or two, exactly what they said in their marriage vows? Many can't tell you because someone else wrote those vows. Some never saw the connection between their vows and their married life. Many discarded them after the honeymoon.

I do a fair amount of consulting work with decision makers, leaders in companies and organizations. I often ask about vision. Usually the leader will point me to a framed poster size statement hung in a prominent place in the corridor outside their office.

When I ask employees about the company vision, few can tell me much about it. I notice the similarity between company vision and marriage vows. We create them in sincerity but rarely integrate them in daily life.

To create a philosophy of marriage you would begin with the idea that it must be worth your time to do it. It will only be worth your time if your philosophy becomes a working philosophy in which you live. Like the idea of a living will which adapts and adjusts to changing conditions, a philosophy that is continually tuned to today's situation, that informs your attitudes during tough times, that carries you through days when you've lost track of your loving – such a philosophy will require some serious thought and work.

A philosophy of marriage specifies the underlying connectedness you share and long for, it is the glue that keeps two people exploring deeper pathways of relating. A little later we'll offer ours – a need-based philosophy of marriage – and you can use it much like sourdough starter in creating *your own.*

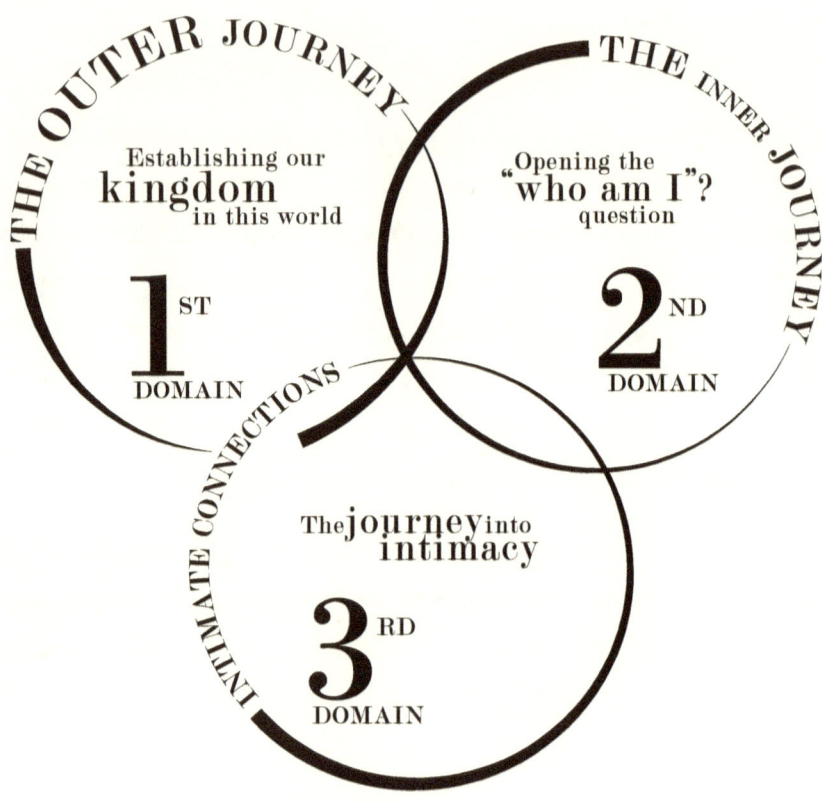

THE OUTER JOURNEY

Establishing our
kingdom
in this world

1ST
DOMAIN

THE INNER JOURNEY

"Opening the
"who am I"?
question

2ND
DOMAIN

INTIMATE CONNECTIONS

The **journey** into
intimacy

3RD
DOMAIN

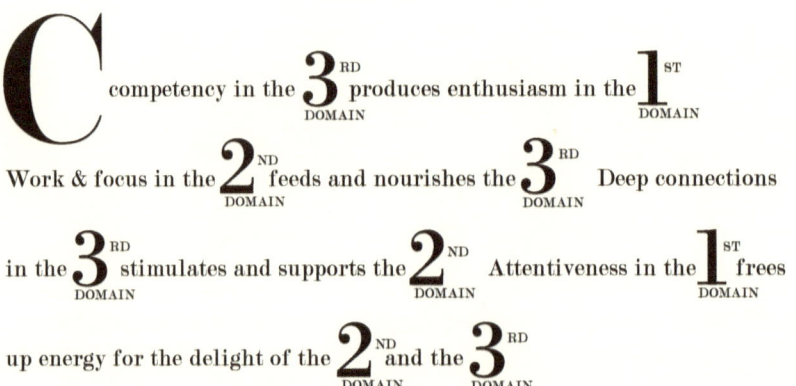

Competency in the **3**RD DOMAIN produces enthusiasm in the **1**ST DOMAIN

Work & focus in the **2**ND DOMAIN feeds and nourishes the **3**RD DOMAIN Deep connections

in the **3**RD DOMAIN stimulates and supports the **2**ND DOMAIN Attentiveness in the **1**ST DOMAIN frees

up energy for the delight of the **2**ND DOMAIN and the **3**RD DOMAIN

2. Philosophy and Journeys: Giving Voice to the Adventures within Marriage

Your life together weaves three journeys into one journey. It could be fun and insightful to try to map your own journeys so we suggest you use our three journeys map to create your own.

Once you begin the adventure, domains become journeys. A description of what your doing (domains) becomes the process of doing it (journeys). The journeys include climate changes, roads not taken, roads taken and abandoned, roads traveled alone and highways shared.

Our map will help you in understanding conflict, opening communication, creating new pathways for intimate relating and move you toward singing new life into your marriage. We think it will. It's up to you to make it happen.

3. Your Personal Garden of Longing and Delight

The third foundation for creating a marriage that sings is the ability to return to your deep love- the love that got it started in the first place.

You'll want to address love's ever-changing, kaleidoscopic, shape-shifting mystery as you create your own model of marriage.

Love's Garden of Eden, born at the beginning of time – your time together – can be easily overgrown with the weeds of disappointment and the inevitability of neglect. Love's foundations need attention, careful consideration, revisiting, tending and vigilance. The slings and arrows of outrageous fortune known to all of us can submerge our genesis under years of debris.

You'll need to create a method of returning and honoring the love that got you started in the first place. And when you do you'll want to visit a garden that's not only well maintained but abundant.

"I love you" must become, over and over again, "I am loving you."

These three – philosophy, journeys and garden – are the foundations for creating a model that will sustain you over time, provide the horsepower for sustainable enthusiasm and open your marriage to the deep resonance of joy and celebration – a celebration you signed up for on your wedding day.

C. What More Do You Want?

"Marriage can work better that you ever imagined," I said. "What's that supposed to mean?" a lean young stockbroker asked at a recent "Marriage Conversation Brainstorm" my wife and I offered to about 20 couples. He went on "My marriage is good. We love each other, have two beautiful children, I think we talk about all the important stuff, we relate as equals, what more is there?"

Good question; what more is there? If we subtract the 50 percent of marriages that fail, and if we ignore the stress, loneliness and adjustment challenges that children of divorce face, and if we overlook the abysmal statistics of second marriages and focus only on the survivors, can we ask, "What more do you want?"

Marginal marriages feed the statistics because they do not really admit that they're not getting to the inner vision they carry for their lives but rarely articulate.

I'm a survivor – a childhood of poverty, of assault, of the deaths of two of my children, of two divorces, of financial failure and more. A few years ago I decided that while surviving is good, I wanted more. When I met my partner now of 25 years, I discovered how little I really knew about what it would take for us to partner successfully. Neither of us wanted another failure.

Marriage isn't meant to be a duty dance in which your love, your creative energies and your capacities for intimate conversation are ignored or given away to others. More likely it is meant to express William Butler Yeats' sentiment, "We must dance and we must sing for we are blessed by everything, and everything we see is blessed."

Marriage is a huge opportunity for individual expression, creative growth, the development of your loving, capacity for conflict, the wonders of partnering and the joys of creating and sharing a vision for your life.

So, to answer the young lean stockbroker's question, I asked him a question. "If you did have a challenge in your marriage, what would it be?"

He looked at his partner then he looked at my partner then glanced at the floor. Hesitating, he said, "I think it would be that she understood my love for her. I don't think she gets how much I love her. And, there are times when I try to tell her," he glances over at her again, "that she just laughs and says 'yeh, me too.'" Finally, turning towards her he said, "I guess I want you to take me more seriously."

I saw a crack in his carefully crafted, sophisticated persona. I saw a quick glimpse of a man, just like me and other men I know, who has a deep need for feeling close, being seen and loved by the one he loves.

To build your own model of marriage, you'll have to accept that marriage challenges aren't all about what's wrong. Many of your marriages work well. We've met you at seminars and workshops. We've seen your love for each other and felt the genuineness with which you honor your partnership.

We've been blessed by your interest in our work, but we think we must expand the marriage conversation because we can expand it. The marriage conversation that most of us are familiar with is pretty limited. The conversation itself has a great deal of room for expansion.

We believe that marriages that do work have a whole lot more possibility in them that is untapped, and we believe our children deserve that we maximize the potential for loving in our families. Pay attention here. Many marriages look good, are functional, and are not on the verge of disaster. Yet, many of these same marriages unexpectedly fall apart. Here's a true story...

II. Marginally Married

Marginal Marriages

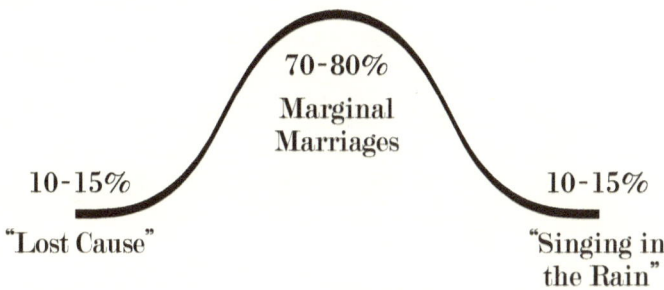

70-80%
Marginal
Marriages

10-15%   10-15%

"Lost Cause"   "Singing in
the Rain"

A couple told their neighbor that they were considering divorce. "How can that be?" the neighbor asked. "You always seem so happy." The couple next door said they didn't know. They just seemed to drift apart. Now that the children were grown they found they had "little in common."

This is a story too often told. When you don't know what you're doing in your marriage it's pretty easy to come up with lame excuses for failure. Truth be told, the couple next door, by any accounts good people, never spent a lot of time tending their marriage.

They did a good job keeping their house clean, driving well-maintained cars, providing for college funds for their children and mowing the lawn. What they didn't do is ask each other what they needed in this marriage. They didn't ask the marriage what *it* needed either.

Marginal marriages are not the same as dysfunctional marriages. Marginal marriages feed the divorce pipeline because when someone in a marginal existence starts waking up to life's possibilities, they are likely to see their partner as the cause of their unhappiness. Marginally conscious people feed marginal marriages.

We say getting your hands around a new paradigm is close to urgent because it will force you to face what you have always taken for granted. A fresh approach, a new model will force you to look your own inattentiveness to your happiness right in the eye.

Here are a few indicators of marginal marriage:

- If you do not share a clear articulated vision for your marriage – it is marginal.

- If you aren't competent in conflict and cannot embrace it, and instead are prone to chronic and repetitive arguments – it is marginal.

- If the light has dimmed, the energy is low and interesting conversation infrequent – it is marginal.

- If you can't tell me, in three minutes time, what your partner cherishes, admires or values about you – it is marginal.

- If intimate conversation – spiritual, emotional, psychological or physical – happens less and less frequently – your marriage is marginal.

- If your vows and commitments are not an integral part of your intimate conversations – your marriage is marginal.

- And, if you can't tell whether your marriage is marginal or not, your marriage is probably marginal.

Let's take a moment and look at these observations:

o *Vision* is not so noticeable in its absence as it is stunning in its presence. Vision pulls you towards something you believe in and are on the way to realizing. Vision gives you lots to talk about. Vision brings juice to ordinary conversations, shapes important decisions and informs complex value-based challenges.

Remember when together you made a big decision, perhaps to move, or change jobs or even to redecorate a room? Remember the new energy that infected your conversations? Vision does that. Vision, in your marriage and about your marriage, changes the energy between you and enlivens every conversation. Later on, we'll offer some "how to's."

o *Conflict* is opportunity though most of us relate to it like it's the plague. Conflict brings the unspoken, avoided, denied, rationalized stuff that is within our relationship and lives between us – to the surface. Conflict offers an opportunity for intimacy by offering a window into each other's shuttered rooms.

o *Being cherished* validates love. Knowledge of our partners, and seeing our partners for who they are requires attentiveness. Later we'll offer a model of what it takes to be intimate with another. But notice, if you are cherishing your partner he or she knows it.

o *Intimate conversations* are defined by three things. First, there is surrender – you make a conscious decision to leave the walls around your city and to meet in the open meadows of unguarded conversation. Second, there is a willingness to listen without bringing an agenda. And, third, there is deep desire to know who your partner is.

Intimate conversations explore, reveal, ask and are characterized by intelligent curiosity. They vastly slow down the usual pace of everyday conversations. Intimate conversations take time.

They also take space. Couples who are competent in creating intimate conversations know they need a kind of space we call a sacred space – a space that is protected from the daily noise of life. They will create a sanctuary – no phones, no TV, no distractions – that can "hold them" as couples as they descend into conversation that will reveal truths long forgotten or truths that are newly emerging.

○ *A working philosophy* means that your vows and commitments are visible in your daily decisions. Vows and commitments aren't traps set to measure your performance or rules to follow in order to avoid punishment. Vows and commitments are expressions of your deepest aspirations, your tenderest affection, your beliefs and your emergent vision. They express inner ideals and, used wisely, are always pulling us toward more competent loving of each other.

A. The Conversation: Invitation to the Dance

I am often told, "Okay, so I think our marriage may be marginal. We're not unhappy but we're obviously not getting all we could out of this marriage. How do we change it?"

The answer is you'll have to have "the conversation." "What's that?" a petite forty-something year old woman said as she scribbled notes in her well-worn journal.

She was bending over in her seat writing furiously. I later learned she was a workshop junkie. She attended everything she could find, read every available self-help book, watched the talk shows, all with the same relentless energy of one determined to get the answers she sought so diligently.

Her husband thought she was kind of nuts and lovingly teased her in a kind of condescending way. "She's got the answers," he said. "All's I got are questions."

They were unhappy as many couples are in a kind of sophisticated, living above it all, way. Neither had affairs, their finances were reasonably well organized and their children were succeeding in school. She wanted more and didn't know quite how to get there. The idea of creating a conversation she hadn't yet tried fascinated her.

I talked a little with them about leadership in relationship. I introduced them to the idea of *natural genius* – the idea that we each bring a gift into this world that is uniquely ours. It can be a way of seeing or it can be a noticing what's missing. Everyone else in the room may not notice that anything is missing, but if your genius is cooking, whatever it is that is missing will be glaringly obvious to you.

In relationships, our petite forty-something woman couldn't help herself. She felt, sensed, imagined that something big was missing for them, and she could not let it go.

Her sense of urgency was magnified by a clear realization of the clock ticking. They weren't getting any younger. Her huge blind spot was this: if something is missing and I'm working as hard and diligently as I can to understand it, then what's missing must be missing in him. I suggested that they create a conversation , a new look at what's going on.

I suggested that they agree to set aside a time without interruption, maybe an hour. That they find a place that's 'safe' – no phones, no children, no distractions – and one that's as quiet as possible.

Each of you will take five or ten minutes to talk about your relationship – what you like, what you see happening, your sense of where you are in this relationship right now. While one of you is talking, the other is listening as carefully as possible, even if you think you know what your partner is going to say. Take notes.

After you've done this, take a break. Walk around a little. Then take another five minutes each. You'll ask your partner what's missing for them in the relationship. You'll each remind yourselves to offer no defense, no analysis and no theories about what's being said.

"What if he says nothing? What if he likes the relationship just the way it is?" she asked. What if he says, "Everything's great. Nothing's missing for me!"

I suggested she try this: "If you *did* have a challenge in this relationship, what would it be?"

The intention of the conversation is to help a couple go beyond stuck. It is to move them into taking individual responsibility for the quality of the relationship. It is to move them away from "we'd have a good relationship if it wasn't for you,

Try to identify the 'conversations' in your marriage that are waiting to happen. These conversations can become the basis for a new style of collaboration in your relationship.

Leadership in relationships looks like two people being willing to imagine better things for both of them. It assumes that neither is functioning fully, both have unmet needs, that there's plenty of love to fuel necessary changes, and that marriage is meant to evolve and grow. To do that, to have that happen in your relationship means you'll have to risk pushing the envelope a little. Leadership, even in its most subtle forms, opens your marriage to new possibilities..

The conversation can be the beginning of real change.

B. Necessary Muscle: Art and Competencies

We all know that to create a conversation that will yield results (positive change) requires willingness, a sense of direction (vision) and competencies. While every marginal marriage I meet is a challenge, every single story I hear of marriage failure disturbs and touches me. If only these couples had gathered a few competencies and if they had a paradigm – a way of imagining marriage that inspired them – they might have made it.

It's not that I believe all broken marriages can be saved, but I do believe many that fail are simply promises aborted. At the very point where real growth would be possible, their marriage ends,

Marginal marriages are dangerous because they do not call for attention the way truly dysfunctional marriages do. Marginally married people are doing ok but they miss the full potentiality that marriage, when imagined more fully or when more fully embraced - offers.

There are necessary competencies you'll need if you choose to go from marginal to magnificent. There are other things you'll need on this amazing journey as well. After we sketch out the luggage you'll need for the three journeys within marriage, we'll be ready to start work on your own philosophy of marriage.

Competencies and luggage will set the stage to start you moving toward creating a marriage that sings..

The second major section of our invitation to creating a new way of relating to marriage will offer several ideas for skills you may want to work on as you build muscle for embracing your marriage.

Remember: We each get to move from monotone (monotonous) to song (tone/ pitch/ rhythm/ lyrics/ melodious) within marriage. It's in your hands. As the old Chinese proverb puts it, "The longest journey begins with a single step."

III. Competencies: The Basics

A. Becoming a Marriage Craftsman

There's a nice little model of competencies that I teach in corporate settings and it goes like this. Every competent person in every effort to fully grasp a skill set goes through four stages on their way to realization of competence.

1. First Level: Unconsciously Incompetent

Think of a young child. Someday they are going to drive an automobile. They will drive in all kinds of weather, on freeways and city streets. They will experience the unexpected, and they will do a good deal of learning on the job.

This child has no idea what tires and wheels are, gas pedals, steering wheel, brake, motor or transmission, much less what an on-board computer does, what traffic signals do or what the myriad rules of the road are about. They don't need to know, not yet.

The child we speak of is unconscious, not aware, of the knowledge and skill she will need to one day drive an automobile out of the driveway. She is incompetent but that is not a judgment. It is an observation.

2. Second Level: Consciously Incompetent

Our child is now a young teenager and is eager to learn all about automobiles so that the magical day when she gets her license will be a joyous one. As she talks to family members, observing how they drive, how they handle unexpected challenges, begins to hear about maintaining an automobile, insurance and all the other things that go along with responsible ownership of an automobile, she will also realize how little she knows.

She has to absorb a great deal of information while simultaneously learning basic driving skills. She is becoming conscious of her incompetence.

3. Third Level: Consciously Competent

Our teenager has been gathering information about cars, she has begun driver's training and is fast learning the skills needed to control the automobile. She will build on that base over a lifetime, but society will establish for her a bar beyond which we will all agree that she is sufficiently competent to drive along side the rest of us.

She will grow in awareness of her competencies and slowly gain confidence to drive in any conditions. Many driving decisions will still be made consciously and intentionally, sometimes making her driving appear awkward.

4. Fourth Level: Unconsciously Competent

One day our student driver will drive to a friend's house and not be aware of how she got there. "I know how to get here so well that I am not even thinking about it." At this competence level she may pass exits on the freeway, skillfully avoid accidents without conscious effort and even adjust her driving for a not-so-conscious driver in another automobile – all on autopilot. She has reached a kind of unconscious competence in which the automobile functions as an extension of her will and intention.

The new hire now handles calls seamlessly, directs traffic effortlessly and represents the persona of the company as if it were his own.

Within marriage, we see clear parallels.

B. Stages and Levels of Competence in Marriage

Now let's take the bare bones model of competencies and look at marriage through the same framework.

1. First Level: Feeding Your Marriage – Facing Unconscious Incompetence

Weddings are parties. They mark the start of something big. They are not the marriage. Marriages require competencies few of us would understand the day we marry. For the most part, we are unconsciously incompetent when we marry.

Don't take offense. It's just that we simply cannot realize the scope of skills, beliefs and challenges to our loving that good marriages present. Most of us do not have much knowledge in these competencies because marriage itself is a "learning community" meant not only for comfort and companionship but also for uncovering, deep sharing and profound growth.

Within marriage we have the possibility of developing our capacity to love.

We may have thought that we loved when we married, and we did. Sort of. Joining in a partnership with another opens new windows – challenges, blind spots, the need for joint vision and more. These new windows call to us for new learning.

Many are interested in marriage education. We see that couples can greatly benefit by being introduced to basic skill sets that are necessary for experiencing deep and lasting intimacy. Marriage education is much needed in a world where we measure the depth of our love by the strength of our hormone rush.

Marriage education however is a little like backpacking classes I've attended offered by local junior colleges or backpacking equipment

Giving Voice to Your Marriage

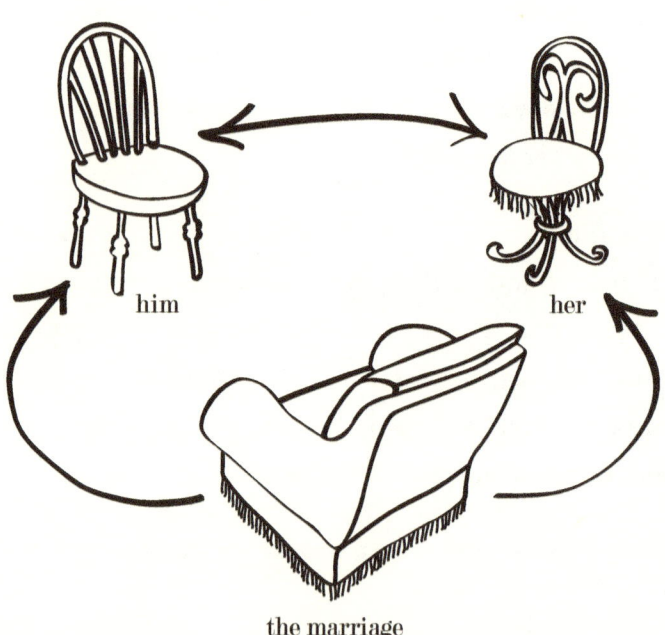

him

her

the marriage

stores. You do get a lot of very useful information but you will not know the kind of challenges you will face until you're on the trail.

So use marriage education as a laboratory, working with your marriage daily as you are learning new skills and gaining new information. If possible take the trail with another couple so that you can together mastermind the changes you're facing.

A couple I coached a few years back was well versed in psychological terminology. They seemed to have mastered the art of labeling their various predicaments. They could recite their issues both personal and as a couple. Still their marriage suffered.

One day I pulled an empty chair over and placed it next to them so that they and the empty chair formed a sort of triangle. I called the empty chair their marriage. I then asked them to talk to their marriage and ask it what it most needed.

Awkward at first, they soon got into it. They started by saying "Well what is it you need, marriage?" And then, "How do we know what you're saying or even if you're listening?"

The marriage was quiet at first. Then Brett, the husband, said, "I hear something inside me. I think the marriage wants to say that we ignore it. That we don't listen to it because we maybe don't know how to listen to it."

His partner, Marisa, was weeping. She said, "I tried to tell you that but you're always busy."

I asked her to speak as if she were the marriage; perhaps Brett could hear her better. Trusting that, they began a dialogue with their marriage and soon were talking about visioning their marriage as they did one night before they married as they stood in a park overlooking the Pacific Ocean in Santa Monica.

They were addressing the unknown and unrealized incompetence they shared. They didn't know their marriage needed to be fed; they didn't realize that they were each 100% responsible for feeding it. They didn't realize that their marriage was also present at the dinner table, in the living room and at the office. This sounds obvious but for many couples it's a common experience.

They were now moving toward conscious incompetence. Here are some indicators that successful couples have given us for beginning the journey from unconscious incompetence to conscious incompetence.

- Recognize that your marriage is an organism and needs nourishment.

- Begin to explore how it might look to gather good information. Start with trusted friends, check out the www. marriageconversation.com website, attend a local workshop or seminar on relationships, go to the self-help section of a good bookstore and browse.

- You might be ready for an initial consultation with a helpful professional – religious advisor, marriage coach, psychological counselor or medical doctor.

- Ask: What would it take to get some traction here?

- Let this awareness in: *Our wedding needs to become a marriage.*

Coaching: Here are a few reminders if you are in a position to be mentoring another couple in their journey towards unconscious competence.

- Recognition of the need for coaching begins with an awareness of distress, absence or lack. It can show up as lack of energy, lack of joy, chronic arguments, boredom and/or distance.

- Stress the importance of commitment to a path. Hold each other accountable for decisions made. Mentoring sometimes works best when the couple being mentored is also working with a professional helper.

- Be mindful that for most of us deep change is glacial in speed. Real growth, real listening, real sharing takes time and so does building the capacities for these skills.

2. Second Level: Agree to Address the Need – The Level of Conscious Incompetence

A very big event in a couple's desire to create a "marriage for keeps" that will last a lifetime is this: You need to make an agreement that honors your need to stay on this path. Opening to the need is not the same as putting your feet on the ground. A good way to do this is to involve a coach or counselor early on.

What is needed? Start with creating *time* and *space* for this conversation. If you have a simple agreement you can start by looking at your individual incompetency. We offer a model in our first book that you'll see in a graphic at the end of this book (**Strengths and Weaknesses in Domains I, II, III**). Use the model to begin conversations.

Remember the 100% rule cautions against mutual diagnosis, analysis, theories about each other and so forth. Focus on your own individual work, not on your partner's. This is a good time to begin journaling your challenges. You'll never see me without a notebook. This is because my own inner work doesn't happen at a set time and place. Inner work happens when it happens, and my notebook/journal is a butterfly net that I use to catch the thoughts and insights that I want to later expand on.

Intentionally reject thoughts or ideas such as "perhaps we made a mistake," "maybe we're just not compatible," or my favorite of all the silly things couples say, "I just fell out of love."

The illusions these clichés point to have nothing to do with the depth of connection you realized at one time and that took you toward the journey of marriage. They are fear-based, they are exit strategies and they are denial writ large.

You will become conscious of your incompetence. Fear is natural and you'll have to look it straight in the eye.

At this level, you are becoming more objective about your relationship. You might say that you've developed enough muscle to take your own relationship on. You may not have much confidence yet, but you have enough to put that third chair in the living room or set a place for your marriage at the table.

Here are some indicators:

- You have begun to identify the most obvious areas of your relationship that need attention.

- Money, sexual complacency or sexual anxiety, chronic arguments, coldness, lack of focus, difficulty in making important decisions, lack of appreciation – these are large yellow caution lights.

- You are on a path to involve a coach, mentor or counselor.

- You both have agreed to take 100% responsibility for the quality of your marriage.

- You are sober about budget, time and individual capacity for inner work.

- Consciously accepted willing to learn

Coaching: If you're able to facilitate a couple at this stage of their work, you are a treasure and a light. Here are some questions that might help them look at their own responsibilities in the marriage:

- Ask: How do you think you "show up" in this marriage? Purposely open-ended, this question can be expanded into the 100% rule – what do you bring to the marriage that makes it difficult for it to thrive?

- What is your underlying philosophy of marriage? What was it when you decided to marry? Who in your family has a similar philosophy?

- What are your most important values today? How do you carry them in this relationship? Are they a cause of intimacy or of conflict?

- What are you each most afraid of?

- How would this marriage look if you both realized your dream marriage?

3. Third Level: Consciously Competent – What It Takes

Getting a sense of how the two of you can live together, work together, support one another and repeatedly find your own pathways to loving each other is a critical indicator of conscious competency.

We'll see this level as "birthing" a focus that began when we talked of listening to your marriage. We'll also call this level – *giving your marriage a voice.*

If you can begin to listen to the needs of your marriage you also can begin to imagine the marriage needing to speak to both of you. This may be a new idea for you. If you can trust it, you'll get lots of fresh information that will help you both embrace the possibilities within your marriage.

Giving your marriage a voice represents a shift away from the self-referencing most of us bring to marriage. We measure the quality of our relationships by images we've borrowed from the media, our parents, and by past wounds as well as the inner ideals we project onto our partners.

Marriage itself has its own ideas of what's needed, what can happen, what should happen and what it is for. These ideas were all present, though you didn't see or hear them, when you approached the altar on your wedding day.

Marriage is a holy and wholesome gift. It is created out of your own deepest spiritual, psychological and emotional instincts, and even the mythic resources of humankind. It mirrors the ongoing cosmic connectedness of the heavens and the earth. This deep longing for partnering not only calls us to enter its mysteries, but also speaks to us as well of its promises. This is the basis for the ecology of your marriage.

Here a couple is slowly awakening to the reality that they are in process of creating a micro-community and that this community lives within, as well as, nourishes and is nourished by the larger communities embracing its existence.

Marriage will speak to you out of your deepest ideals, your most profound spiritual instincts and the shared values of your chosen communities. The voice of your marriage is not to be ignored.

Here are several indicators of movement into *conscious competence* within your marriage:

- You begin to listen to your partner as if she/he is speaking for the marriage as well as for herself.

- You have sketched out a plan for dealing with your losses and wounds and for going forward into your ideals.

- You agree on what and how to focus your work together.

- You both begin journaling this new approach to your journey.

- Your marriage begins to have a voice, a presence and a distinct reality in your daily living.

- There is a spirit of cooperative exploration.

- You have gained familiarity with the "three marriages" within marriage.

- Conflict is naturally and effectively embraced and replaces chronic arguments, combativeness and mean spirited competition.

- Your "dreamed" marriage begins to be visible.

Coaching: Coaching a couple at this level will look more and more like collaboration. There will be a mutuality of sharing, leadership will shift according to natural genius (we'll look at natural genius and its effects on the relationship later) and accountability.

- Ask: Who are you? Then ask: Who do you want to be for him/her?

- Ask: What are you most afraid of?

- Invite deep disclosures of spiritual questions and insights, psychological terrain, and images and fantasies that have been kept hidden from one another.

4. Fourth Level: Unconsciously Competent – The Courage to be Partners

In order for a structure to be built which will support the marriage through countless changes and challenges, a new definition – profound not minimal – will be needed that will hold you to increasing levels of responsibility and commitment.

Why? Marriages do not become marginal because people are stupid or because they don't love one another. They slide toward marginal because a clear ideal is not continuously calling to them. Their definition of marriage was marginal to begin with and they never addressed it. Here, on the fourth level of competence, it is imperative that you address what it is you need, want, have to give and believe about your marriage.

We call this level unconscious competence because you no longer appear to be working at the relationship. Instead your "work" has become a natural part of your love and the joy you experience is a natural consequence of that work.

Here are a few summary indicators of unconscious competence in marriage:

- Marriage is believable at a new level.

- Your relationship is experienced as a "working lab" for your loving. It is a work in progress, never arrived at, always calling for your attention.

- The One Hundred Percent rule is fully and naturally embraced.

- Personal ego is no longer driving conflict.

- Personal authority feeds the relationship.

- Deep empathy is present.

- The wedding is now becoming a marriage.

Coaching: Collaboration, visioning, inviting other couples into the conversation – all are present in this level of coaching.

- We now begin to notice and define the presence of the "orphan" in each of us.

- The "beloved daughter" and the "beloved son" are archetypes present and fuel your conversations and challenges.

- We look at the legitimacy of our own loving.

- We look to create "sacred space" and "sacred time" for explorating and discovering new dimensions to our love.

- Poetry, good literature, theater, music and art are identified and explored as tributary streams for the nourishment of your marriage.

5. Fifth Level: Embracing the Community – Conscious Loving at work.

With the mastery of the skills of competent roommates, with the juice that flows from an active life of inner work and the deep satisfaction that comes with living frequently within the journey into intimacy, you are ready for service.

Does it surprise you to think of your marriage as more than the satisfaction of your immediate needs? There's been a great deal of attention given to the roadblocks, wounds and frustrations of partnering. Much of that has been helpful but without a profound paradigm to call us on to service that attention may become narcissistic.

Here are some indicators of living consciously while embracing community:

- Your marriage is your art form.

- Symbolically and actually your marriage calls others towards relational excellence.

- You see the possibility of coaching others.

- Your marriage is an asset to your community.

- Creativity and vitality are apparent.

- Your journey into intimacy looks like, sounds like and feels like a garden.

- Leadership shifts between you according to need and the presence of natural genius.

- Your own extended family is healthier because of your presence.

- You bring balance, wisdom, inspiration and good authority to your community.

- You've taken the indicators of a marginal marriage and turned them all into positive statements.

Coaching: We look for mentors to the mentors.

- What does this marriage now want to be?

- You are extending your awareness to full appreciation of core values of your partner.

- Curiosity has replaced criticism.

- Leadership shows up as a question: What's best for this marriage, this family and this community?

- You are mentors in action.

- Conflict, together with expanded openness, enlivens and enriches your relationship and that of others. No end in sight.

- Your marriage has become a learning community.

IV. The Three Journeys Traveling Guide

You have stayed with us as we established the groundwork for taking your marriage from marginal to magnificent. We looked at indicators of a marginal marriage, and we offered a model through which you can look at your own competencies in marriage. Now, try out the language that we offer there. Use it to initiate conversations about the quality of your relationship.

To create a bigger picture, one that can invite you into continual exploration and ongoing curiosity about the infinite possibilities within your relationship, you'll need to reconsider how you think about marriage.

A. Create a Map

Remember the young lean stockbroker? He thought he and his partner were doing fine and they were – by the only standards he thought about at that time. But when we offered a "map" that would introduce new possibilities, he was interested.

We told him and the other couples gathered that they'd each have to do a little preliminary work. We'd have to know where they now "lived." Not physically, but relationally. How do you deal with money, we asked. What does your shared vision look like? What are the most evident emotional challenges you face? How does conflict show up? Tell us about the frequency and vitality of intimate conversation in your relationship.

It might look like this. "I live with constant worry about money. My partner, though, lives as if there's always plenty of money."

We'd call this "conflicted perceptions street."

"I imagine that we need to save money rather than spend it on stuff we want to do right now, and she sees that we're young and we'll have plenty of opportunity to save later."

Their address would be "headed for trouble" on conflicted perceptions street. The background music will be the blues.

Of course, we're playing with an idea here. I want new pathways, new ideas, I want to experiment with my honey and continually bring the needs of this marriage out into the open.

In order to get your hands around this, try creating a map. It would include a clear statement about your values as well as an attempt to locate where each of you "live."

You might want to brainstorm your financial destination, including how you see yourselves living in three, five, and 10 years. Conflict will be natural to this dialogue. You'll want to practice trusting by treating each other *as if* you have *their* best interests at heart.

"As if" means you risk letting go of your 20/20 diagnosis of your partner's shortcomings.

Now the map. Put it on paper. Name the streets or highways. The "I have no idea how to think about this" road. Or, the "impossible dream" highway. Mark the milestones of change, the "we agreed on a three-year plan" hotel, or the "our paths diverge here and we need help" bus stop.

A good map would picture the imagined scenery on the way– mountains (what obstacles do we face as we envision our lives), rivers to cross, rest stops and calamitous events. You should list your challenges (separately) and keep them handy. List where you'll need more information and where you'll need a guide.

Most important, have fun. Mess it up. Try different maps. Leave them around the house. Write on hers, put ideas on his. I want you to create a little distance from the intensity of your mutual analysis and in its place try to own/ invent/ or imagine a new conversation about the way you live in your marriage.

B. The Journeys Tell You Where You Are

Let me refresh your memory (if you've already read *With These Rings*) or let me introduce you to another way to view relationship challenges. We see that you can nicely lay out the challenges of marriage by seeing first that there are three domains to focus on.

Each domain contains within it, a journey. Domains describe the content; journeys describe the action.

*1. Once we decide to partner we become **roommates**.* Whether or not we are competent roommates is a question we all must address but clearly, basic skills are needed here, for example, how we deal with *money* – budgets, earnings, allocations, planning, etc. Competencies here tell us a great deal about the success of our partnership.

How we deal with *space* – your space, my space, our space – interior and exterior decorating, space to entertain, space for our family. Living together within a space you define and honor has a great deal to do with attitudes towards your own inner space.

Space is alive with the possibilities of relationship.

We know that being comfortable in your own space is fundamental to a healthy relationship. It is burdensome to live with someone who is unaware and therefore not respectful of personal space.

And there's *time* – schedules, your time, my time, our time, leisure and recreation, speak volumes about boundaries, sensitivity to one another and appreciation for your partner's individuality.

The idea of consciously chosen time in which you concentrate on the quality of your life together is an indicator of the presence or absence of empathy in relationship. Can you see how that works?

These quick summaries give you starting points as you think about mapping your marriage.. They are descriptions of the first domain, the "world" of roommates. We can easily dumb down this world with poor management of resources, petty arguments about money or time or just plain old disinterest.

But, this domain becomes a challenging journey if you can expand your imagination to include the building of a 'kingdom' (yours), and begin to see that time and space are relational gifts as well as descriptive of your needs. The first journey begins to come alive and looks like a shared vision for life on this earth.

Why does life within this journey so often become contaminated by chronic arguments? Is it because many have lost the connection between, for example, money and love, or space and tenderness?

The first journey offers the possibility of adventures along the way, unexpected detours and possible calamities. We could have a Strauss waltz here or, perhaps, a little Wagner.

It's a journey because neither of you fully knows the path – none of us really do - the outcome or final destination. Journey speaks to your willingness to share the discoveries as well as the work that surely lies ahead. Imagining work with time, space and money as a journey changes the language you use in daily discourse. It can turn an argument about money into an exploration of needs, capacities, vision and love.

Thinking of roommates as a journey becomes an invitation to transform ordinary arguments into lively sharing.

2. Notice this: you have a robust inner journey going on at the same time you're living as roommates. Many couples, not realizing this, tend to become dull or flat emotionally. In our culture, we address this flatness or dullness by offering toys, trips and addictive substances. These rarely bring new life to a relationship.

Your *inner world* contains the real life drama of your personal history (the impact and ongoing influence of things you learned early in life). Your inner world contains the answer to the "Who am I?" question. There's abundant information available through dreams, fantasies and images. Some move us to anger or toward tears, others inspire and invite new work.

While we might say that religious practices reveal a lot about our outer commitments, our spiritual lives, far subtler and many times more difficult to calibrate, are values and commitments of the deepest possible level of ourselves. *We can safely say a person's religious practices may not reveal at all just who that person is spiritually while their spiritual life will be evident in the way they live and relate to others.*

Emotional I.Q. describes how well we know what we feel, how integrated it is with feeling knowledge and how competent we are in communicating this powerful dimension of our inner world. The world of our emotional life includes getting a sense of the feminine side for men and the masculine side for women. Your creativity, aspirations, deeply held values and beliefs all live here.

A woman I coach said recently, "I feel I have two voices going on in my head." I said, "Probably more like an entire theatrical company." Our inner worlds are busy places populated with voices, many of which we don't recognize as our own.

Without a rich inner life and a serious intention to explore and confront your own inner voices, and without well-developed communication competencies, life flattens out, relationships suffer and everyday looks a lot like yesterday.

3. *The journey into intimate connection* contains all the "juice" that *gets us talking about marriage in the first place.* Its richness depends entirely on the quality of consciousness you bring to your own inner journey. If you neglect your own inner work, life in the first domain (as roommates) will be reduced to budgets and dishes. And, life in this third domain will be reduced to viagra and the cosmetics of intimacy.

Neglecting the substance of who you are when you're trying to get to intimate relating (the promise that drew you together in the first place) is a disaster in the making.

Without self-knowledge, access to humility and deep feeling, you really have nothing to bring to intimacy.

Pay very good attention to this. Without willingness to mine the gold you have within coupled with a profound sense of your own inner journey, what you bring to a desire for intimate conversation, is as shallow as it is cold.

The journey into intimacy, when two responsive and response-able people partner in this desire, is at the same time the Grand Central Station of relationship and the journey to the Shangri-La of our dreams.

This third domain contains the alchemy of lovers bringing their ordinary substance, their 'base metals' if you will, into the cauldron of discovery, exploration, revelation where transformation is possible

Within the heat of deep disclosure driven by a kind of holy curiosity, we change and our loving evolves.

Our relationship, if only on the roommate level, becomes not much more than an ordinary, even if cherished, friendship. If, on the other hand, we are eager explorers of our inner world and have no knowledge of the third journey, we may become self absorbed, perhaps insightful but ultimately barren partners.

The journey into intimacy is a journey of invitation, encounter and deep joining. Invite your partner out of the daily world and into serious conversation. Take the elevator down a floor. You'll find adventure here – consideration of who you are spiritually, exploration of your own and your partner's unique psychology and an uncovering of the emotional terrain you operate within every day but perhaps fail to expose to the one you live with.

Physical intimacy within this third journey takes you beyond the sex manuals with their focus on performance and technique. In the journey into intimacy, you'll want to know about the physicality of your partner, his aches and pains, her rhythms, challenges and images of pleasure.

We called this a cauldron of discovery because the biological and chemical changes that result from true and genuine exploration create a kind of reenactment of the creative process. The third journey turns up the heat. We can live as roommates and keep our cool because the language of roommates is mostly logical and rational, but we lose our cool in the third journey and we do so intentionally.

By the way, we've come to see that the heat of this journey warms both your life as roommates and your desire to know more of who you really are. All three journeys interact with, inform and enliven each other.

Within true intimacy we see changes in our partners. Also, their interest, curiosity and loving change us. This really is the heart of my belief in the need for and possibility of life long commitment.

Without time together in which life itself "calmly gives out its own secrets," (Rilke) we only touch the surface of our own possibilities. Only in the last decade have I begun to seriously explore the quality and genuineness of my own loving. Without a life partner that would be impossible.

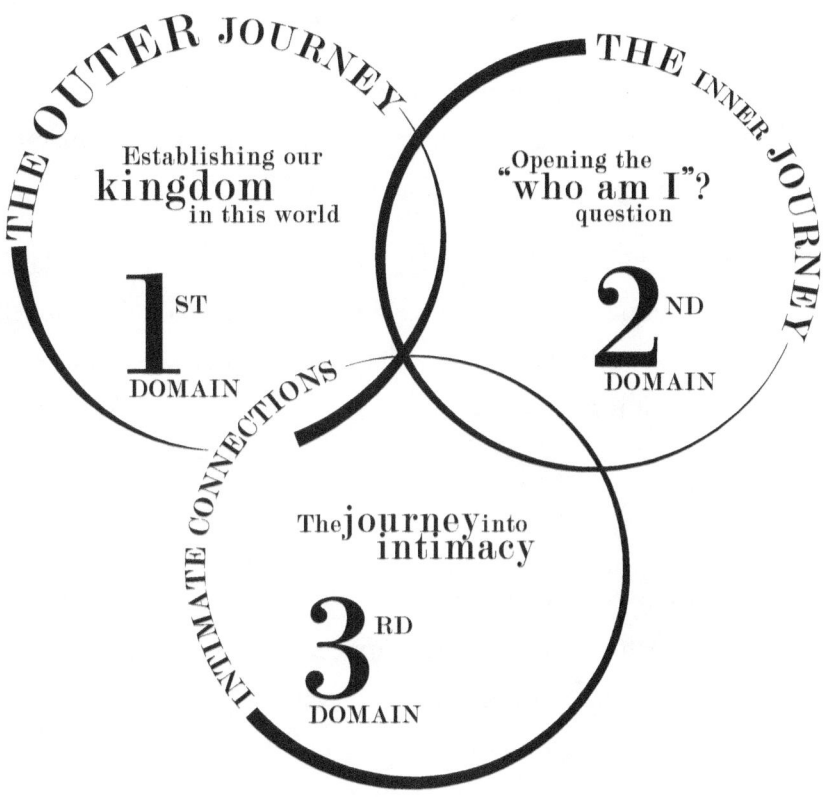

THE OUTER JOURNEY

THE INNER JOURNEY

INTIMATE CONNECTIONS

Establishing our
kingdom
in this world

1ST
DOMAIN

"Opening the
"who am I"?
question

2ND
DOMAIN

The **journey** into
intimacy

3RD
DOMAIN

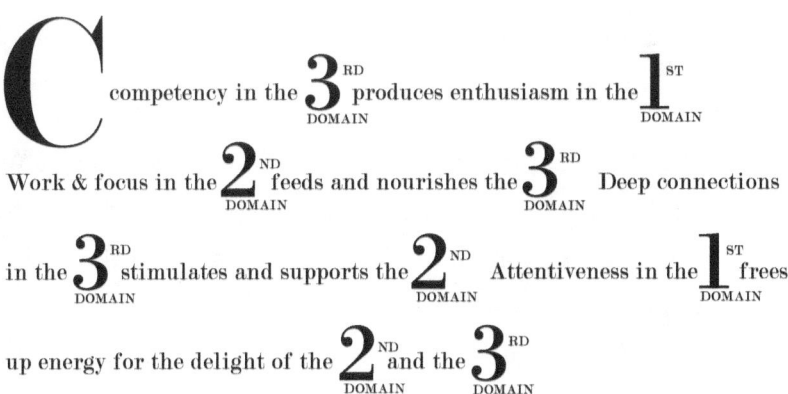

Competency in the **3**RD DOMAIN produces enthusiasm in the **1**ST DOMAIN

Work & focus in the **2**ND DOMAIN feeds and nourishes the **3**RD DOMAIN Deep connections

in the **3**RD DOMAIN stimulates and supports the **2**ND DOMAIN Attentiveness in the **1**ST DOMAIN frees

up energy for the delight of the **2**ND DOMAIN and the **3**RD DOMAIN

C. Mapping

As you begin creating a map for your own journeys you should realize that the idea of journeys is a device to help you get started imagining what you're doing together and to start doing it differently.

If you buy into this way of recreating joy and intimacy in your relationship here are some tips to help you. Later we'll take a look at luggage you might want to leave home and luggage you'll need as you journey into the space of intimacy realized.

Tips

3. Listen to your partner as though for the first time. The powerful idea here is *curiosity*. Listen to how he talks about his life, suspending judgment, theories, speculation, all you've learned in psychology classes and so on. If she complains about being out of shape, for instance, or he complains about money, your job is simply to record it. Listen in, as they say. Find a place within yourself that is interested, curious and loving. Nothing more is required.

4. We like to use the idea of brainstorming the journeys. What could your outer world (first domain) look like in three months, six months or a year if you followed the path you desire? Have fun. Draw a timeline on your map. Create rewards for reaching milestones you think are possible. Include time outs for mini- vacations. Perhaps a small reward for the hard work of being accountable to each other.

5. Pay attention to the importance of acceptance and forgiveness. If you are truly experimenting with a new way to imagine your relationship you'll need to have a sense of humor and an awareness that you are as big a doofus as your partner is.

6. We ask each person to create a map for themselves and then one for their partner. No looking over the shoulder on this second one. Let the creative process happen. Remember, everything can evolve and change. We're simply opening the doors to creative exploration.

When you have something, even rough, put it on the wall where you both can look at it for a few days. No analysis allowed. The only words that are acceptable as a response to your partner's map are wow, and "I never knew that" and "Really?"

Use the maps to stimulate further conversation about challenges, discoveries, feelings and intentions. Never to criticize, demean or theorize about your partner.

Now let's take a quick look at luggage.

The film critic, Pauline Kael, offered this when asked how she managed to maintain balance in writing her movie reviews: "I sit in the center of the theater. Too far down, and I'm too emotionally involved, too far back and I'm too objective. I have to find a space where I'm involved and objective – the center of the theater..."

D. Luggage

There's baggage you'll want to leave behind. For example, in order to explore the journey into intimacy you'll want to abandon all ideas of who's right and who's wrong. You'll also want to leave your diagnostic spectacles behind – as in "the trouble with you is..."

Freud liked to say that, "When two people married, six get into the bed." Leave your parents behind. They were good or bad or a combination of both, but in this exercise you'll want to un-invite them. You'll need to make a conscious decision that there's no one to please. You'll need to give up the longing for applause.

You'll replace this baggage with a new sense of determination to create the marriage you already have within you. You were born with a deep sense of how it might be for you, and this work is meant to fully reveal that to you.

Over-packing for any journey is burdensome. Some easily discardable items include these: suspiciousness, competition, whining, preening, gathering evidence for your case, living with past wounds, worrying about the future and the need for entertainment.

Make your marriage your project. Decide to give yourself fully to its successful realization.

A woman I know had a long history of failure with men. Her childhood was awful, and it included the violent death (in her presence) of her father when she was a very small child.

Over the years she developed a style of performing for the men she chose. She got their attention and enchanted them with her considerable charm. Men could easily fall in love with this amazing apparition.

Soon they were proposing, full of desire and also some sense of how they might save her from herself.

When I met her, marriage number five was disintegrating. She had married a bright, resourceful engineer. He was a commonsense kind of guy who, it appeared, genuinely loved her. He came to a coaching session focused on work in the third journey. First thing he said was "This is impossible. When I try to relate to her she either gets scared, backs up and runs away, or she starts one of her old numbers. I've seen them all and they no longer interest me."

You might say she knew what worked and so she carried her "tricks" around as if in a suitcase. They were old tricks, created when she needed them to survive. She no longer needed them but hadn't yet faced that truth. This husband would be the one to help her through that painful process.

Some married men drag cute little tricks that worked with their mothers. Their wives make jokes about them when talking with other women. The tricks may be harmless but that's part of the problem. Men who use their old devices in relating to their mother may be cute but their partners will never know them for who they are behind the masks of accommodation. What worked with mother rarely facilitates intimacy with your partner.

In the language of our culture, Peter Pan will have to leave the lost boys to their own devices, give up his fascination with Captain Hook, and start paying attention to Wendy.

Leaving unnecessary baggage behind frees you to shop in new stores, try different things on, and experiment with who you are today. Right now. Right here.

If you limit the baggage you bring into the journeys you are about to begin, you might ask what is necessary in the larger journey into conscious partnering.

E. What You'll Need on the Journey into Intimacy

Every traveler knows what she needs in order to be comfortable. But taking an uncharted journey into the world of soul and spirit is another matter. You have to be open to the unexpected, travel as light as possible, and have a willingness to develop competencies along the way.

You'll have to know what interests you and what doesn't, and you'll have to risk discovering new interests. If I pack for a journey heavy on arguing over fine distinctions about the meaning of love, I'll be heavily weighted intellectually but there will be little energy for play.

What interests you in intimate conversation should be clear to you. The decisions you make will carry your intentions. Clear intentions are one of the aphrodisiacs of intimacy.

You'll want to pack extra pairs of patient listening. You'll need an extra supply of curiosity mixed with a conscious awareness of who your partner is – today.

A good skill to pack is this: Start each day fresh, trying as best you can to forget all you know about your partner and to discover him as if for the first time. And here's its corollary, "Live each day as if it were your last."

Finally, bring along an open heart, a strong memory of who you love, a commitment to continually deepen your own love and a willingness to be loved.

F. The Big Picture

Why do so many couples look dazed? Why do they sit in restaurants and stare out the windows as if alone? Why have marriages that started out full of excitement, anticipation, celebration and certainty turned into dull conversations where every day looks and sounds a lot like yesterday?

A favorite movie of mine is *Terms of Endearment* with Jack Nicholson playing an aging astronaut and Shirley MacLaine playing the woman he loves. The scene that stopped me because it resonated was the beach scene. They have parked their convertible on the beach and Jack is looking skyward reminiscing about his days in space. He says, wistfully, "That was my moment."

Shirley's character listens, and then looking at him tenderly says, "This is my moment."

He looked back; she embraced the present. Living there she invites him into a new way to experience love. Whether you're in the first domain and looking at redesigning the living room or taking a vacation, staying present in the present will take you away from old baggage that simply isn't useful anymore.

I introduced With These Rings *in this way: "my mother lived in the past – 'she should have married Gus'; and in the future – 'some day I'll be with*

Jesus.' What she couldn't do is live in the present, in her marriage to my father. I was her youngest son."

Marriage lived in the present mysteriously comes alive. Pay attention to the subtle ways you both reference the past or the future. Begin coaching each other on what's going on right now. Within the inner world of discovery there is always an invitation waiting. You may have to wear your old decoder ring to stay in touch with it.

Invitations to exploration come from surprising places. Recently I sat in my study staring at the computer screen for a long time before I realized I was stuck in a zombie-like state in which the enchantment came from my lack of purpose. I had no idea what the morning offered or what I was doing there.

I got up, went outside and walked to the shed. Inside was a bright red cultivator I bought several years ago on sale. Outside my study window was a patch of ground covered in weeds.

I fired up the cultivator, walked around the yard and over to the patch outside my study window. Not ready yet with a conscious purpose, I began cultivating the long dormant earth. As the warm sun bathed my body I came alive with the purpose of work. An hour later, sweat drenched, I knew what it was I wanted to write at the computer that morning.

The invitation to discovery was hidden in my need to move, to get my body living again. In a similar way, some of the best conversations in our marriage happen when we're doing something else. We only need to recognize the invitation to discovery to take full advantage of the moment.

At a recent workshop a woman said this as we talked about discovery. "That all may be true, but you'd have to have a partner that's interested."

We stopped everything right there. I asked "Is your partner not interested in who you are?" He was sitting next to her and was quite eager to answer. She answered first. "He may be but all his time is spent in his books, at his computer or watching sports. There's little time for exploration of anything with us."

I waited a moment and he said, "Can I contribute to this? She says I'm not interested in her but I am. What I'm not so interested in is the gossip about her family, her tracking of the lives of the rich and famous and her gripes about our neighbors. That stuff bores me. If she was really talking about herself – yourself," he said as he turned to her, "then I would listen. And, I would be interested."

"This can be a big conversation in itself," I said. "What's needed is a conversation about the kind of conversation you'd both like to have. We frame this as an invitation because we've seen that all truly intimate conversations happen by invitation, though of course not a formal one. There needs to be present a clear sense of where you want to go, of willingness – yours and hers – and even a space where it's safe for it to happen. We try, when we can, to schedule time where we will not easily be interrupted, and often we bring some healthy snacks."

The young man might consider asking his wife what she likes so much about the rich and famous and why it is that they so interest her. He might take a look at his judgmental attitude and also look at the quality of conversation he brings to her. We introduced them to the 100% rule that afternoon and gave them some exercises to begin a new style of conversation.

And, on the other hand, she would do well to "reality test" her assumptions. We'll present a model a little later on called CAPPS that demonstrates how deadly assumptions can be and that opens a fresh pathway for getting to intimacy in conversation.

In order for an invitation to be compelling, you'll have to tune into your own agenda. Ask yourself: "what am I most afraid of?" "who do I think my partner is?" and "who do I want to be for them?" If you are clear with yourself you'll be able to show genuine curiosity about your partner.

Marriage as an adventure waits for you to embrace it. Your marriage has needs you can easily ignore. Give your marriage a voice, tune into it and your conversations will begin to change.

The dazed couples we mentioned earlier may simply have lost track of the amazing, interesting, always evolving person sitting right in front of them. Remembering that is one pathway to the genesis of your love. Your personal Garden of Eden, the love garden uncontaminated by life's disappointments, personal wounds, losses and failures is a place of repose where your deepest love for each other waits your attention. That garden is alive and well beneath the debris you've allowed to obscure it.

Following the next couple of sections on competencies and caution, we'll return to that garden as we look at the idea of transformation.

This seems to me like a good place to explore your belief system about marriage and relationships. I'm going to offer our working philosophy of marriage because it holds us in commitment and supports our intentions to continually move forward in relationship. In doing this,

I'm hoping to inspire you to look at the thought/ belief basis for your marriage.

Ask yourselves:

- What is it that my partner most needs?

- How do I really approach conflict?

- Am I more concerned about being loved than I am about loving?

- What does my history tell me concerning big changes in my life?

- What is my most common feeling/state?

V. Creating a Philosophy of Marriage

Competency in relationship requires an allegiance to a bigger picture of marriage than the one you now have. That's presumptuous, I know. But many people when challenged to give a simple statement of their philosophy of marriage, don't give much back. I imagine most marriages walk around with a too small idea of the possibilities within.

Competency requires new images, a fresh look at your needs. It requires you to entertain the possibility that there's more – much, much more – to be discovered within each other than you've ever dreamed possible. A philosophy of marriage will help you do that.

We know that relationships over time lose energy. Some of you become comfortable with the patterns you've created and, since those patterns are efficient, as well as familiar (familial), you can live within them without challenging them.

The good thing about patterns is that they help us get things done, help us to predict and live within comfortable expectations. Marginal marriages are pattern dominant, however, so we have to consider that some patterns are also dangerous within relationship.

Competencies are best built when patterns are challenged. When talking of a personal disaster it's not uncommon to hear a person saying things like this: "That was the best thing that ever happened to me."

They say this because a personal disaster creates havoc with familiar patterns. We are thrown into a steep learning curve. We may doubt we can survive it or doubt we can do what it takes. And then we do and are amazed, looking back, at how much we've changed and grown through the experience. We need challenge and change within stability and trust.

A good and useful philosophy of marriage will offer principles and guidelines that anticipate the many detours on your journey together. It will offer a belief and value base that you can return to when lost, sort of like your own personal GPS.

Marriage is a promised land of meaning, joy, growth, sharing and contribution. We all signed on for more happiness and fulfillment than we did for loss and sorrow. Yet loss and sorrow come with the package.

Here's a story. I left home at thirteen and a half years old. I found my way to a farm in eastern Pennsylvania and was hired on by a family who took me into their hearts and home. I learned to work on this five hundred acre farm.

We milked eighty to one hundred Holstein cows each day, bred the young stock and raised their calves, cared for their health and managed their food. I learned to handle a tractor, plow, harrow, mower, rake and bailer, handling every piece of farm machinery as we planted and harvested the grasses we grew for hay.

We had a converted Army amphibious vehicle (called a Duck) that we used to plow snow in the winter and pick rocks off the fields in the fall. I mastered that truck as well as many other farm related skills. .

The farm was well equipped with every kind of machinery needed, and at fourteen and fifteen years old I learned to handle all of it. We even had a Piper Cub airplane that we used to fly to farm auctions. I learned to fly that plane solo and had a great deal of fun doing it.

My boss's name was George and we became as close as father and son. He taught me to drive, fly and handle and repair all kinds of machinery. He also taught me to discern the qualities of soil, the care and husbandry of animals, and the variations in plants and grasses.

In summer we spent fourteen to fifteen hour days together milking the cows, mowing, baling and gathering the hay for winter and putting up silage. As my interest in girls began to show, he gently coached me in the ways of men and women.

George came into my life at the time when young men need older males to initiate, guide and show them how to be men. He was a wonderful teacher and friend, but as I approached sixteen things began to change. I missed my family and wanted to try living at home again. On a holiday weekend home, my oldest brother unexpectedly came home from a two-year tour of duty in the army. Seeing him again after all that time away, I was overwhelmed with my love for him and his for me. I decided right there to leave the farm and move home.

George was devastated when I told him. He was so angry that he wouldn't even talk to me. I was incompetent to explain, give him notice or in any other way lighten the impact of my decision. Clearly, I handled it poorly.

I visited George a few times over the next couple of years and on my second visit, perhaps two years after I left, he and his wife had a new infant son. They were in their mid forties and didn't expect to have any more children. Yet there he was with a new son. I was surprised by it then. I am not surprised by it now.

The loss of our friendship and partnership had opened the way, I think, for new life in his life. I could not be the son he so longed for and he could not be the father I needed, though we both tried to make that happen.

What we need most is often far from what we think we want. We live a good part of our lives creating patterns that give us the illusion of meeting our needs. Yet most of us walk around with a deep sense of longing, and we can't quite identify just what it is we need.

I believe that creating an effective and lasting relationship is need-based. You'll have to do a bit of work to identify just what (for you) those needs are. I'll offer seven principles that, in our marriage, form our value foundation. They are need-based principles and, if you look at them carefully, they point to a strategy for meeting each need.

These needs are basic to all humans but when seen in the context of creating healthy relationships they appear as guides for centering, focusing and connecting to the one you love regardless of circumstance.

A. A Coherent Philosophy of Marriage: The Need to Love

I know this: to tell you that the first principle in a needs-based philosophy of marriage is the need to love doesn't make it happen. Not for me, not for my partner. Our past learning is very strong here. We habitually focus on what we've focused on most of our post childhood years – and that is the question of *whether* we are loved or not.

SEVEN PRINCIPLES FOR TRANSFORMING MARRIAGE

- The Need to Love. And the Need to have our Loving Received

- The Need to be Seen

- The Need for Growth and Change, And the Need for Stability

- The Need for Conflict

- The Need for Commitment

- The Need for Conscious Communication

- The Need to Share ourselves Intimately with Another

The challenge *to love* is easily lost. Negativity creeps in. Competitiveness summons us. "What about her?" we ask. "She paid so little attention to me last week at the neighbor's party." "He laughs at the dumb things Heather was saying and gives one word responses to my attempts to connect with him."

Surely "we'd have a great relationship if it weren't for him/her." The strategy of staying away from your own loving by focusing on a diagnosis of your partner's loving (or lack of it) maybe works as a survival strategy in childhood when you could see with 360 degree vision who loved and who didn't. But it doesn't work now.

This is, perhaps, man's best-kept secret. I know a family who emphasize that children should respect their parents above all else. In a recent conversation with the mother of this family I complimented her eleven-year-old daughter for having a good sense of her own authority. Mom replied this way, "That's all well and good but she has to respect her elders."

Perhaps without realizing it, this mother is teaching her children a value system that endangers them. In this world being grounded in one's own authority is fundamental not only to grounding your loving but also your safety, well being and your success in life.

Personal authority and the capacity to love are bedfellows. They go hand in hand. They support each other as well. If I am grounded in my own authority, my loving you means something.

If I focus on my loving rather than on being loved, I'll consistently and continuously deepen my connection to my own authority, genuineness and legitimacy.

Loving is the "coin of the realm" in families. Here's what the Apostle Paul says of love:

I can speak with the eloquence of an angel, but if I'm not loving, I'm like a noisy brass band or an inconsequential tingling of a cymbal.

And, if I can correctly see into the future, and can understand complex and daunting mysteries and even am the smartest person I know, and on top of this I have a very positive attitude and deep faith – yet without the capacity to love, I am nothing.

If I am generous to a fault, and I'm willing to sacrifice my life for the good, and have no love, I am nothing

And then he offers this, *Love is patient and kind. Not jealous or boastful, not arrogant or rude. Love doesn't insist on being loved, isn't irritable or resentful. Love doesn't rejoice in someone else being wrong but (instead) rejoices in the right outcome. Love can bear all things, believe in the best, live exuberantly in hope, endure the worst. It never ends.*

... when I was childish, I spoke in a childish manner, I thought in a self-centered way, I reasoned from the point of view of my own selfishness. But now... I give up my childishness. Now, I am ready to love.

So it is that there is faith, hope and love, all three. But the greatest of these is love.

(This is my own translation of I Corinthians 13 of the New Testament.)

The first principle of a healthy marriage is first because nothing else works if you cannot love. Everything hinges on your willingness to face your own limitations, your own deceits, heal your own wounds and change the entire paradigm under which you have lived.

Notice this, too. The culture in which you live will not be of much help here. It will point you towards your rights or urge you to fulfill your individual wants. Even your spouse may discourage you by acting out your projections. Projections? She/he is probably more like you than you think. If you are focused on being loved instead of loving there's a good chance that your spouse is doing the same.

To build character, try loving those around you. Deciding to love can seem daunting. "How can I when he/she is so…?" Moving through your anger, penetrating your fear, turning your back on your history of wounds and losses, transforming them by consciously loving – will change your life. All this you can begin by embracing the marriage that started you on this path.

Caveat: As I'm talking about loving, I am aware that some may mistake this for a false idea. I'm not talking here about chronically abusive relationships. I'm not suggesting that you accept any form of abuse or that you try to love an abusive partner into loving you. There are highly dysfunctional, diagnostically mentally ill people. If you are in such a relationship, get professional help immediately.

I am talking to those of you who I like to call "healthy neurotics." I am one myself. Here's a story.

At one very low point in my own inner work, I struggled with whether I even had the right to live. I wasn't yet consciously suicidal, but my thoughts and mood put me in the danger zone. I simply couldn't tell at that point whether I ever loved anyone, and I certainly couldn't feel love from or for anyone. No one, that is, except my youngest son.

One day as I was leaving a session with my wonderful, kind and wise therapist, he said as I opened the door, "Don't forget your love for Andrew." I knew I loved this son, yet those words became sustenance for me.

Each day, regardless of how dull and unloving I felt, I would go to my love for him, and that would become a beacon of light. Of course I loved all my children, but that youngest son touched the most tender and undefended part of me. That love penetrated the darkness of my depression.

I was moving between unconscious incompetence and conscious competence. My own wounds were so severe that I hadn't yet penetrated the layer of protective debris covering them. I could not move around in my loving without triggering fear of betrayal and fear of huge loss.

My numbness covered my love and my loving of Andrew gave me a light so that I could move forward.

A need-based philosophy of marriage honors your own work and can lend a hand in your desire to become fully functional in your loving. It will offer a structure within which you can work, Your deciding to focus on your own loving will lead to consideration of new vows as well as new starting points leading to intimate conversations.

I believe our need to love is biological. Our bodies need to love as much as they need oxygen. When I feel tired and listless and my work isn't going well, I go outside, do some heavy work – wood chopping or tending the garden – and in minutes my energy is restored.

Love is like that. It is not meant to be stagnant but always wants to be moving. In fact, a better image might be that of flowing. Love, like the water of life, becomes unhealthy when it's stopped up, contaminated by negativity or misdirected into false desire.

Love and the need to love are spiritually essential. Our longing to *know* love is met by our willingness *to* love. We become how we show up. Living within your loving, looking for ways to express it, withholding your criteria of who deserves it and who doesn't, leaving your fascination with old wounds behind – all this is spiritual work.

Why is that so? Our fundamental challenge in life, before anything else can happen, is to move from acting like, believing in, or hanging out in an *orphan psychology*. The need to be genuine translates into believing you are legitimate, and legitimacy shows up as the capacity to love.

Loving has no agenda, is not looking for approval and doesn't focus on tit for tat. Love believes the best about others and, in marriage, is always looking for an opportunity to flow. Love withheld is like a river damned by debris; its abundant life-giving resources sicken, the lands beyond dry up and become infertile.

To love another breaks the bands of self-protectiveness we have so carefully built around our hearts. Loving not only feeds the other, it feeds the one loving.

Distance from your loving looks like abandonment, abuse, shame, neglect and isolation. Making a conscious decision to love has immense curative powers. A good little book to look at is W. Mitchell's *It's Not What Happened to You But What you do About It That Matters.*

Secondary to your need to love, of course, is the need to have your loving received. Notice I didn't say the need to be loved. The core competency of loving another will stand whether or not your loving is received, but having your loving received completes the loop and legitimizes your partnership.

Remember the young lean stockbroker? He wanted his partner to be aware that something was missing in the reception of his love. Be careful here. This observation could easily become a criticism or diagnosis. While he could and would go on loving her, their relationship would start to sing if he could feel her receptors opening. And, he just might have to learn more about his loving once she received what he brought to her.

We can choose to become available to being loved, thereby transcending our well-constructed defenses learned a long time ago in a land far away. This is one basis for hope in relationship.

If loving is essential to my own sense of legitimacy, then change within our relationship is not far behind.

B. The Need for Stability – The Need for Growth and Change

Conflict is a powerful change agent. We need change because it points toward the challenges of the future and fine-tunes us within the dissonance of the present. A relationship is always dynamic, and each individual within a relationship is continuously changing as the relationship grows and deepens.

What the young lean stockbroker knew was he wanted change. Not to change her. Change. He wanted what chiropractors call an adjustment. But it was an adjustment of attitude, and if successful, one that would bring them closer together.

Some relationships begin to fall apart when one of the partners experiences a "growth spurt." I wrote a little piece on just that when my ten-year-old daughter seemingly overnight went from fairies and gnomes to preteen questioning of everything I said. (You can read it at www. marriageconversation.com.) We could easily have gotten stuck in a kind of power struggle there. Many parents and children do and they carry the power struggle on into and throughout adolescence. But her mother and I recognized the need – her need – for change and growth. We began to talk together about this new developmental stage as well as our own triggers, fears and competencies.

We needed some stability in our relationship with this daughter and at the same time we needed to honor her evolving sense of herself. A big order.

We're often not aware that change has been brewing for some time. One day it hits us as the next new thing. From one point of view there have been changes going on which if looked at closely would have alerted us to the more dramatic experience of change that surprised us.

It might look like this in a marriage: you've seen a show and been touched deeply by something one of the principles said or did. Or, you've read an article that got you thinking in a new direction. Maybe a friend recently told you of his or her decision to divorce or someone you love unexpectedly died.

These seemingly unrelated events got you thinking about mortality, quality of life, even the nature of your loving. This inner processing then shows up as a new attitude. You don't sound like the person you once were. And, of course, you're not. Something new and fresh is manifesting in you and because it is yours you take it as natural that your partner sees the world the way you are now seeing it as well.

It is natural to resist change because we rely on stability for predictability and therefore efficiency. It's nice to have some routines, to know what to expect, to know who you're talking to. Change can be unsettling.

Joseph Campbell does an exceptional job of framing the "hero's journey" as a journey in embracing change. It is really the embrace of life itself because, as the philosopher Heraclitus noted a long time ago, "The only thing that doesn't change is change itself."

Some psychologists, years ago, developed a theory of "hardiness" and two of the three indicators were the ability to embrace change and see it as good, and the acceptance of failure as inevitable. Failure is simply an opportunity for growth.

Robust relationships create enough stability to provide comfort and a certain level of predictability while at the same time exposing, exploring, discovering each new manifestation of their own unique individuality.

Our bodies are always changing and so our relationships – contracting, expanding, shape-shifting, stabilizing and giving us plenty of occasion for intimate exploration.

Commitment, permanence, predictability and routine all hold us in this cauldron of life. And, in reality, both change and stability are somewhat illusory themselves. What we have, as Eckhart Tolle eloquently reminds us in *The Power of Now*, is the eternal present.

It may be a good idea to think of change as a gift of life and your loving as the force that keeps you reconnecting in the now of it all.

Behind the awareness of change, however, is another fundamental need.

C. The Need to Be Seen

We never outgrow our need for visibility. While the culture focuses on how we appear on the outside, our need to be seen has far more to do with people seeing our inside – our intentions, our good will, our effort and our challenges.

A man I know well chronically complained about the skateboarders who hung out at the local mall. They were noisy, dressed outrageously and frightened many people. These early teenagers slalomed in and out of the crowds scaring mothers with small children, the elderly and handicapped while scarring up the wooden benches and scraping the paint off the newly painted red curb.

One day he told me this: "Last week as I walked from my car toward the supermarket, I was suddenly struck by the grace and agility of two boys who were on their skateboards happily jumping on and off the red curb. As I walked toward the door of the supermarket, one of the boys who had a full head of steam going, jumped, pirouetted, jumped again and then stopped in front of me balancing his entire body on one end of the board – kind of like a flamingo on one leg. I said, 'Wow! That's beautiful!' He turned towards me, his face glowing, 'Thanks man,' and skated off.

"His response to my response changed my attitude towards these young men. Full of energy and often a nuisance, their performances are also their work of art. I began wondering about the skateboarder within me and if I had only seen them as a nuisance because I resented my own lack of joy and self-expression."

There were many things in this man's life that he wanted "seen" by those he loved – his own amazing and subtle acts of kindness, his willingness to help others, his skill problem solving. He didn't feel particularly seen by others and he was noticing that he hadn't spent much time "seeing" others.

A three year old when telling you about a flower they just discovered or about a bee buzzing in the garden – lights up when you stop, look and listen. This need is strong and it grows stronger over the years of our lives.

Here's how I first learned about the pain of not being seen myself. Years ago as I walked in my neighborhood I was surprised by a discovery. There was a jeep for sale – red with chrome wheels – and it was well within my means to buy it. I'd wanted a jeep since I was 13 years old. Still do. When I lived on the farm in Pennsylvania my boss had a jeep. He taught me to drive it and from there I learned to drive every piece of farm machinery he owned. The jeep introduced me to a whole new world. I would take it out in the long summer evenings, driving out over the pastures and meadows and through the woods of the farm using it to bring the cows in for milking. On Sunday afternoons, my day off, I'd take the jeep over to my neighbor's farm where my friend Joe lived. He and I did a lot of exploring in that jeep.

When, years later, I saw a red jeep for sale I was delighted. Later that day it so happened that I was having coffee with a woman friend. I told her about the jeep. My excitement was over the top. I also told her that it was financially feasible and perhaps I would pursue buying it. At that point I noticed she was not interested in my jeep story. Instead, she looked at me with a blank face and with a voice flattened by boredom, said "My, how you do ramble on."

She could not see me. Her interest was elsewhere. Perhaps she had deep concerns of her own. And, before you say it or even think it – I know. *It's not all about you, Stephen.*

Yet this experience stands out not because I suddenly discovered just how narcissistic I am or can be. I know that. It stands out because in that one "pure" sharing moment I experienced another person's total disinterest.

The need to be heard and the need to be seen by those we invest ourselves in relationally is huge. It can be, but it is not the same as "it's all about me." It is about a deep mutual respect, attentiveness and genuine curiosity. *That* is the essence of loving.

D. The Need for Conflict

Funny how this need is greeted in workshops. People will virtually howl, "We need less conflict, not more!" Or, "We argue all the time. I thought we'd learn here how to argue less."

Conflict is an underappreciated gift in relationship. It's underappreciated because we don't understand what it's there for. If you argue all the time, you are not enjoying the gift of conflict. Chronic arguments are conversation stoppers, power plays or unwitting distance makers.

If you really want to know someone, and there's trust between you so that they risk exposing their true attitudes, feelings and "outside the box" thoughts – the contours of their inner landscape – you can be sure conflict is just around the corner.

We see a need for conflict and that need, if embraced, will neutralize arguments. Better, it will not so much neutralize arguments as honor the substance and delete the drama that characterizes arguments. Arguments, as we are using the term here, are loaded with *inner* conflict which is easy to put on your partner as diagnosis or analysis of them.

Relationally, conflict is underappreciated. Two people living together change with the daily rising of the sun. Some changes are subtle and go unnoticed, others are noticed but, perhaps, we lack the skill or the will to talk about them. Still other changes frighten us so that we want to bury them someplace where we will not have to look at them.

Inevitably, individuals will grow and change and the change will show up maybe as a mood, maybe as withdrawal or, perhaps, as an angry attitude. Soon argument over something trivial will occur.

What happens is this. We're annoyed because our partner is loose in the shoes about money. We haven't yet accepted Dr. Bruce Derman's critical observation *We'd Have a Great Relationship If It Wasn't for You.* Here it is: "you're more alike than you're not alike."

Derman teaches that what brought you together was commonality but not only of "we like the same kinds of movies" sort. Your neurotic styles, your bozoness, your blind spots – all have more in common than you suppose. Arguments occur when you "can see the speck in your brother's eye, but can't see the two by four in your own." This translates into a good deal of self-righteous grandstanding. Arguments don't go anywhere because you're yelling at yourself and not admitting it. You haven't yet accepted the 100% rule.

Conflict is not argumentation. Conflict exposes self-revelation. Conflict involves self-disclosure. *Conflict is driven by a need for real change.* Here's some background for understanding conflict.

Two individuals are on their own pathway. They are growing, changing, learning. Ideally, each is becoming more fully the person they are meant to be. In domain one, a person is growing in his understanding of and relationship to personal space, money and the awareness of time (which all relate to an appreciation of mortality – but that discussion is for another time).

Each person in the relationship is also living a sort of double life. The outer person being a kind of agent for the twin who lives within. This inner journey we dubbed domain two. It is a journey of depth and takes us into exploration of the impact of our childhood, our spiritual uniqueness and quest, the topography of our emotional life and our changing physical presence.

Domain two is the domain of the hero, the fool, the guru and the lover. What shows up in the world, however, shows up in our roommate journey (I) and the journey we got married for in the first place (III), the journey into intimacy.

This brief reminder of the core of the *With These Rings* model, takes us toward understanding why conflict is so crucial to healthy relationships. Conflict is the juice that supports the exposure of real change.

True, healthy conflict isn't about what's wrong with your partner. It isn't about how difficult they are, how messy or irresponsible they can be.

Conflict takes the substance of your work in the inner journey and brings it into the light of day. Its presumptions are: love, curiosity, truth, needs, empathy, presence and deep relating. Here's a closer look at these ingredients of conflict:

Love. When you come towards your partner with an emerging awareness of changing needs you come with the legitimate expectation that not only do you love that person but also that you are loved. This belief sets the context for healthy conflict. Your loving (for example, your truth) may not look like or sound like love to your partner.

Curiosity. Good conflict supposes that your partner is interested in what you have to say and why it's important at this time to say it. You are curious about each other's inner worlds. While arguments are power-based and look like attacks, good conflict looks like "we got some course changing to do and you are the one and the only one I want to do it with." Curiosity isn't always greeted with applause.

Truth. I believe that you love me. I believe that I love you as well. Perfect love speaks the truth. But truth is somewhat relative to the truth teller. When your truth doesn't resonate with your partner's truth, the opportunity for discovery is greatest.

Needs. The seven principles that we're proposing as a basis for a philosophy of marriage are based on need awareness. We intend to sponsor or encourage a growing awareness of individual needs in a relationship. This is to be distinguished from wants, as in "I need a new car," or "I need to have an affair."

Needs are fundamental to humans. We need to eat, sleep, exercise and create. We also need to love, have our loving received, share ourselves, communicate and more. Of course we need to conflict because conflict exposes where we are as compared to where we like to say we are. Conflict keeps us in reality as well as in the present. Notice that your needs are essential to conflict and form a sort of gift to your partner. They provide a pathway to understanding 'what's needed' here..

Empathy. To feel with your partner is an act of loving – to stand next to him and not change him, to listen to her resonance and not criticize it. To empathize is to imagine who your partner is without belittling, competing with or shaming them.

Presence. Conflict is different than argument in another important way. When arguing we are not present. We are, you might say, possessed. We are in the grip of a shaming demon, or we are in a superior stance that has nothing to do with love. We may be re-enacting a childhood wounding or trying to repay an earlier slight in the relationship. Whatever it is we're doing, it isn't (the truth test of conflict) *in the direction of becoming more intimate.* Presence starts with awareness. "This is who I love. This is the one I've chosen to be with." This awareness grounds the coming exploration that we're calling conflict.

Deep Relating. Conflict is not like argument because it takes us into our own deep truth, and down into our soul. Conflict is meant to open a new path, perhaps unfamiliar, of understanding, loving and deep connection. Conflict is to be welcomed, embraced, celebrated for without it you really don't have much of a relationship. Do not confuse it with arguing, competing, posturing, shaming or struggling for power. *Conflict's gift is a pathway to more intimacy.* If it isn't serving that goal, it shouldn't be called conflict.

E. The Need for Commitment

Conflict's partner is commitment. Possibly one reason we are conflict phobic is that we haven't had much experience with the "staying power" of others when faced with conflict.

My daughter Jennifer was in third grade when she was deeply hurt by another little girl. I was between careers and was making a living painting houses while awaiting my next revelation.

One afternoon as I pulled in the driveway, tired and dirty after a long day's work, Jennifer came running out to my truck, tears streaming down her face. "What's wrong?" I said as I climbed out of the truck. "I feel that Sophie doesn't like me," she sobbed.

We walked together into the house and into her room where, sprawled on her bed she told me the story. Her best friend Sophie had lately seemed indifferent to her and that day stopped talking to her. She wouldn't play with her and ignored her the entire day.

I was in my first year of psychotherapy and naturally offered advice. I said, "Did you tell Sophie how you feel?" "No," she said. "Well, why don't you tell her how you feel about how she's acting?" This thought hadn't occurred to her and she brightened up. "Okay, Daddy," she said. Her sorrow lifted. The rest of the evening went fine.

The next day I was anxious to get home to hear how it went. When I pulled into the driveway, out she came running even more full of tears or so it seemed. I said, "What happened?" She sputtered, sobbed and said between bouts of grief "I – said – to – Sophie, Sophie, I feel like you don't like me anymore, and Sophie said, 'That's right, Jennifer, I don't like you!'"

The evening was long and sorrowful. I felt terrible. My advice had produced the opposite of what I'd hoped for. *Maybe,* I thought, *Truth isn't such a good thing after all.*

The next day she was on my mind all day. I wondered how she was handling Sophie's rejection. My heart was heavy for her. That evening I pulled into the driveway anticipating her sorrow. But I didn't see her.

I went into the house and there she was playing on the living room floor. I tentatively inquired, "How'd it go today?" "Fine," she replied. I paused, then tried again. "I mean with Sophie."

"Oh, we played together. We're best friends again," she said as she continued playing.

We can see that "best friends" never stopped for Jennifer and Sophie, they simply took a short break. Anxiety will take you towards fear. You can begin blaming, projecting, adjusting and adapting until you've abandoned all idea of friendship altogether. The friendship, for a moment, forgot about commitment.

The necessary presence of conflict in relationship raises the need for awareness of commitment – hers and mine.

Remember that you're a lifer: Whatever this current situation looks like I'm not bailing out. We're angry and we have a right to be, but neither of us is going anywhere.

Commitment creates a space where the relationship can grow. Commitment specifies the rules of the game – we're in it for life; you and I both are always changing; conflict is natural and necessary and has gold hidden within it; and, our job is to love each other.

Commitment reminds us both that we believe in something far deeper than our present fear and anxiety might indicate. And, commitment holds us to perspective – it is based on the roots or basis of our loving and it resonates to that energy. The capacity to reconnect to what we call our personal genesis – our garden of delight – is indicative of couples who allow their relationship to become their art form.

At the deepest and truest level, commitment is really about commitment to oneself. It is commitment to my own choice of partner, commitment to my loving her, commitment to a standard, which says, "I commit to be faithful to myself, my choices, my belief in my love and my loving."

F. The Need for Communication

If there is to be change, growth and conflict, there will also be a corresponding need for commitment and that need opens to the need for communication. We are never exactly the same person we were an hour ago. Neither is our partner. If only that were the case, the challenge of knowing each other would be difficult. In addition to our continual changing, everything around us is changing, as well. Our children, parents, relatives, neighbors, colleagues and mentors – all are continually morphing into their own next manifestation. The environment, climate, economy and world situation are all constantly changing. In this swirling, noisy cauldron of change, communication with those you love is critical.

We usually think of words as primary vehicles of communication. And they are fundamental. But we communicate in many other ways. Everything we do communicates. The way we work with time, for example, exposes our priorities. Space and the way we share it, live in it and create it exposes the presence (or absence) of personal boundaries, empathy, even values.

Money is a great communicator of how we see and are seen by those we love. What we do here, our awareness of attitudes, our decisions and priorities, the openness and willingness we bring to shared goals, the articulation of vision – all communicate with a power that exceeds mere words.

Conflict is the midwife of communication. So is sexual intimacy. When we embrace the mutuality of both partners needs, we embrace a broad range of possibilities for lively and powerful communication.

Many couples operate on a narrow bandwidth. They restrict, withhold, deny and avoid potentially painful subjects because they fear their love will not be sufficient to "carry the day." In doing so they lose a lot. They are unwittingly creating a "closed mind" ambience in their relationship that soon shows up as boredom or worse.

Communication, an always expanding art, requires that you consciously face your fears, deepen your loving, risk being hurt or hurting your partner, engage in exploratories, reveal tender spots, confess ignorance, check your ego, and drop your weapons – other than that, it's easy.

Communication and community have the same root and carry the idea of sharing our lives with others. Be alert to the culture you live in – entertainment, easy solutions, sound bites and quick fixes. Many are in danger of replacing all real communication with a breezy and superficial style. Some cope with all uncertainties by turning up the volume on the television.

We need more incentive to talk with one another not less. Remember, the number one skill in effective communicating in any relationship is genuine curiosity. To create the possibility of real communication with each other takes time, disciplined interest and love.

It may take hundreds of words to explain your point of view, but only a few to say "tell me more" and "I love you."

Finally, we saved the most powerful piece of a philosophy of marriage for last.

G. The Need to Share Ourselves Intimately with Another

To be seen, to love another, embrace conflict, live with inevitable change and communicate in a real-time manner, to create stability as you both grow and do all this in the context of reliable and dependable commitment – these are the necessities and luxuries of healthy relationships.

We long to share ourselves. Today, I'm working in the garden. Warm sun and soft breezes on this spring California afternoon. My partner shows up with a glass of iced tea and a nonchalant "How's it going?" It was a gentle and innocent question but underneath it I could feel her love. Something inside woke up. I soon felt the excitement of sharing the work I was doing. While I was working I was thinking about our family and the harvest we would enjoy together in the months ahead. My working in the garden, good for me and deeply enjoyable in itself was also a deep expression of my love.

Pathways to Intimacy

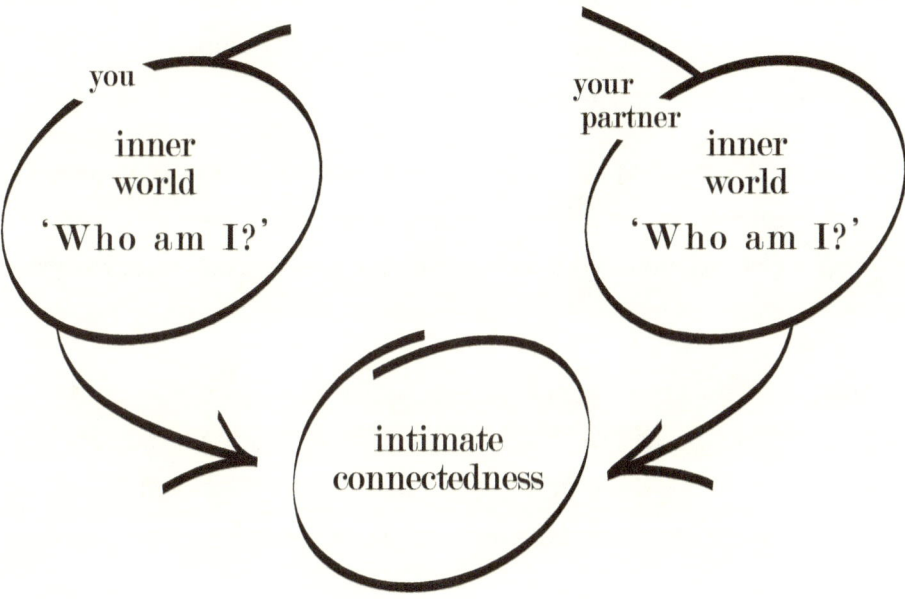

We can't wait for a "date night" to share these simple moments or a Valentine's Day dinner to express our love. If we do, most of what we bring to the relationship will be lost.

I sat at a meeting of the local Chamber of Commerce some months ago and the conversation at our table drifted into relationship talk. One of the women, nervously I thought, laughed at the impossibility of getting her husband to listen to anything she said. "All he does is work and watch TV," she said. "I guess it's his right to relax when he comes home, but I work too, I'm tired, but I relax by sharing. The TV doesn't relax me."

The other women at the table laughed but there was a palatable sense that the reality of the TV watching, non-listening and hard working husband, though painfully familiar, wasn't a joke at all. No one mentioned that some women had given up on their own relational authority and so saw no way they could possibly impact these "lost" husbands.

They weren't aware that intimate conversation requires the competency to create delicious invitations. Possibly all they knew was passive compliance or dead end arguments – neither a very attractive alternative.

Sharing ourselves intimately takes consciousness, competency and work. A man I know trembled when he was faced with telling his wife in my office that he was afraid his company was going to fail. He had withheld this information for a long time fearing she would ridicule him or worse, compare him unfavorably to other successful men in their social group.

He was surprised when she reached over, held his hand and looking into his tearing eyes said, "I don't care if we have to live in an apartment and have only one car between us. I can go back to work. I don't want you under this much stress."

That evening we did a great deal of work on the nature of partnerships. We looked at patterns in their parent's marriages, opened conversations they'd been afraid to have, talked about how their withholding the more painful and frightening issues from each other had affected their sexual intimacy and even "connected the dots" to some challenges they were having with their teenage children.

My love for you is a hot Saturday afternoon mowing the lawn and sweeping the driveway. It's the knot in my stomach when you're out later than expected; it's the hanging up of the bath towel you left crumpled on the floor.

We see that a needs-based philosophy of marriage is really an invitation to talk about who you are, what you value and what you need – together and often. You'll need skills and competencies to do that. You'll need to surrender to the reality that each of you has made the best possible choice in choosing each other. No need to look anywhere else, no need for an exit strategy. You have exactly who you need. All you have to do is claim them.

VI. Dream Realization: Marriages that Sing

A. Looking Towards What's Ahead

In a lovely new book by Michael Meade, *The World Behind the World*, Meade talks of the thread that connects the mind to the heart. It is also the song that keeps or attends the rhythm of our life. This thread, ancient in origin, also exists, I believe, between lovers once they've laid claim to the possibilities of their love.

Marriages sing because an individual's heart knowledge resonates and they enjoy the competence to know when dissonance is present. Competence means not only recognizing the dissonant music born of change, human differences, misunderstanding, projections – anything that separates, but also the skill, ability and willingness to take that information and heat it, purify it and shape it into gold. That is the power of conflict embraced.

This gold is the gold of your own inner and natural genius, your original spiritual, psychological and emotional fingerprint, with which you gift your partner. The gold is the alchemical combining of ordinary human substance transformed by the power of conscious loving.

Two individuals may take a lifetime to mine this gold and to offer back to humankind the riches that brought them together in the first place. For not only did we mate with the possibility of procreating and extending the human race, but we were part of a deeper purpose which can be expressed as *gifting the wisdom of your journeys together to others*. This song will be sung for generations to come. Or its dissonance will be passed on to the children's children until one couple embraces the challenge of hearing once again the songs of the ancestors.

The song is the song of loving, a song where children are safe, communities are productive, the swords of darkness are beaten into the plowshares of health, fecundity, and purpose. A "kingdom on earth" in which we celebrate living and our deepest longings are realized.

We're going to take these lofty ideals and put feet under them in this section. We'll look at the competency of self-worth as seen through a simple model of self-esteem that I developed some years ago.

Self-worth can be and should be used to frame the idea of this marriage. We're interested in not only your individual self-esteem, but in the self-worth of your marriage. We ask, "What does this marriage think of the way you live it?" Additionally, you will learn to take self-worth and apply it to the discovery of your own natural genius.

As an appendix, we'll introduce a word of caution. We offer four "song killers" along with four alternatives that will help you bring the song back into your marriage.

There are other goodies coming. A quick look at learning to listen even for those who believe they already are good listeners. Along with that we'll give you the newly created and exciting CAPPS Course on listening with purpose.

There is a section on the disciplines required for those who seek excellence in marriage, a section on leadership and marriage, and throughout some encouragement on how to stay centered as you embark on an entirely new way of embracing the promise inherent in the words spoken so long ago – "I do."

Yes, we have work to do but I know of no project more worthy of your dedicated attention. Personally, I know the price of failure – as they say in Memphis, "Been there, done that, got the t-shirt."

The best investment I have ever made in my financial well being, business success, self worth as a man and father and more, is the investment of time, energy and money that I have made in this marriage.

VII. The Marriage Conversation

I was in Napa Valley, California, working to understand exactly why I had traveled hundreds of miles to spend long intensive days with sixteen people from around the world learning a new language of leadership. My coaches were warm, informed, even brilliant and they expected a lot from us.

One day I asked Marsha Shank, coach extraordinaire, something about the rules, asking for a breakdown of the day. I was from an academic (clinical psychology and divinity studies) background. What I wanted was a kind of syllabus to orient my day. She looked at me as if I were walking on the moon.

"The leadership conversation is about forgetting all you've been taught and learning a new paradigm for framing the challenges of leadership," she said, or something close to that. Leadership conversation? What possibly could that mean?

It was the beginning of a major reframe for me and it naturally spread to my interest in marriage. I couldn't see that there had been much that was new in framing the challenges around marriage though, of course, there was a great deal of excellent work around relationship competencies. I decided to take a long look at "The Marriage Conversation." Here's where that went.

Paradigms

We live within paradigms. Paradigms are models of reality that shape the way we learn, influence our perceptions and frame important issues.

Paradigms are the architectural design creating the building before the building is built. How that building is used, how it "shows up' is specified by the parameters of its design.

Currently, marriage is considered within a patched together and basically worn out paradigm. It looks to me like 12ᵗʰ century romance, 15ᵗʰ century property protection and a 20ᵗʰ century party called the wedding. Obviously, this is an over simplification but so is most of our talk about marriage.

In fact, marriage is so oversimplified that most of us cannot answer this question: What does marriage add to a relationship? Or this: If a couple genuinely loves one another, honor their love with fidelity and are committed to share their lives together, how would marrying change their relationship?

You see the challenge. In Western Europe each year fewer couples are bothering to marry because they cannot answer these questions to their satisfaction. Here in the US, that trend is also beginning to take hold with an additional twist. Those that are marrying are postponing it to later in life.

Most of the public debate focuses on divorce. But divorce would dramatically decrease if our picture or our idea of marriage was compelling.

Why is this important? If you're reading this book you have an interest in the specific ways marriage might be healthy, might add value to your life and, perhaps, might add value to the world. I do as well so we have a lot in common.

The marriage conversation contains the value added conversation. It also contains strategies for maximizing the possibilities within marriage. The **Three Journeys** and the **Three Marriages** within those journeys are paradigmatic. They are ways of perceiving possibilities, strategies, expectations and the embrace of challenges.

Introducing a **Philosophy of Marriage** supports a serious consideration of what relationship, over time, and within marriage, is for. And the centrality of your **personal Garden of Eden**, the root of your love grounds the entire enterprise in purpose and resolve.

The word marriage changes the game.

A. Skills and Tools Necessary to Claiming Your Marriage

Life within the Marriage Conversation

Before we introduce some skills and tools essential to realizing your dreamed marriage, we invite you to do a little audit.

If your relationship is "working" and you are content with the level of intimacy you experience, if conflict brings you closer and your vision is consciously shared in both domain one (roommates) and three (intimacy), and if you are comfortable with your goals and philosophy – then perhaps new challenges aren't going to interest you.

However, here's a surprising truth: We aren't meant to coast, to arrive and to achieve relationship perfection. Being in a relationship is a gift that keeps on giving if you embrace it. A relationship is dynamic. It is a shape changer, always moving, growing and changing. Relationships changes as we change and our changes are re-imagined as we choose to relate. The changes become something and the something itself changes in response to the changes we are continually confronted with.

> There's a beautiful little poem that includes these lines:
> you come near me with the nearness of sleep.
> And yet I am not quiet.
> It is to be broken.
> It is to be torn open.
> It is not to be reached and come to rest in ever.
> I turn against you, I break from you, I turn to you.
> We hurt, and are hurt, and have each other for healing.
> It is healing. It is never whole.
>
> (Wendell Berry, "Marriage")

So to consider the idea of necessary competencies, you may want to first consider the value you place on yourself – your self-orientation so to speak, and the value you place on your partnership. You may want to join me in a little imaginal exercise.

B. Starting at the Center

Years ago I was fortunate to have the privilege of working with a very conservative Catholic woman. In psychological language, she suffered from low self-esteem. She worked at a Catholic Retreat House and was mentally abused by her boss, the head sister.

She had also been abused by her ex-husband and, in addition, had few skills to cope with the demands of modern society. She had a very sensitive and beautiful way of seeing others. She didn't judge them. She tried to understand their point of view even when being abused.

One day as she told me of her attempt to help a fellow employee who was also struggling with an abusive boss, some words out of the New Testament came to me. The story of Jesus contains striking insights into finding your own value and worth if you can hear it not as a sermon but as story.

The words that came to me were the words spoken by God about Jesus. The clouds opened, it is said, and a voice spoke, "This is my beloved son in whom I am well pleased." I allowed myself to editorialize and spoke those words out loud like this: This is my beloved daughter in whom I am well pleased. She looked at me and virtually collapsed in grief. I cried, too, as we both realized a temporal situation had been transcended. In that moment the universe itself confirmed her beloved-ness, her value, her legitimacy.

Some months later I invited 40 or 50 women to a workshop. I called it "The Beloved Daughter Workshop." We focused on accessing legitimacy and used the story of Rapunzel, an abandoned daughter, to frame our work.

At the center of each of us there is a legitimate child. We might say that alongside that child lives another, one not so sure of herself. She often acts like an orphan. She gives her power away to others, doesn't realize her gifts, minimizes the value of her loving.

We're healthy when we can touch the legitimate one within and relate out from her center. We're in trouble when the orphan is in charge.

I, of course, am not talking about biological parents. It can be said that many children who experienced abandonment at birth are solidly connected to their legitimacy just as many children raised with their birth parents struggle with feeling like orphans. Instead, I am attempting to convey an image that is strongly felt but rarely identified in many people.

Legitimacy

What do these two personalities look like? The legitimate inner child:

- knows he belongs,

- accepts that she is loved,

- feels the right to be who they are,

- stands up for what they believe in,

- is free to love,

- isn't intimidated by someone else's rules,

- will not accept abuse,

- is able to be productive with any chosen task,

- is more collaborative than competitive,

- listens empathically

- and leads as if it were natural to them.

The Orphan

The orphan:

- struggles with purpose

- can't find his center

- looks to appease others

- searches for applause

- is rule bound or insensitive to society's limitations

- tends to stay in adolescence

- accepts abuse as beyond their control

- loves conditionally

- is plagued by moods

- is hyperactive or walks around with little energy.

To work toward entering the marriage conversation it would be a good idea to inventory where you are in the orphan/legitimate conversation. I sometimes have asked leaders to create an orphan page in their notebook faced with a legitimate page. Then I ask them to enter every indication of these two states that they can identify as they go about their work.

To be legitimate in this world is to know deep within that you belong. Orphans apologize for being in the world (or sometimes attack the world for not accepting them). Orphans vacillate, procrastinate and tell half-truths (or, are rigid, inflexible and doctrinaire). When you're an orphan you complain about your partner to your friends and hold back your truth when you're home (or, you relentlessly attack your partner and deny your own responsibility in relationship failure).

I know I'm legitimate when I fully expect that my partner wants to hear what I have to say, when I don't recoil from conflict but instead view her position empathetically without losing my own point of view. Legitimate partners, you might say, act with emotional intelligence.

These two caricatures will be further sharpened up in our look at self-esteem. Before we do that I want to suggest some questions for you to ask each other.

- What's missing for you in this relationship?

- What is it you most need in this relationship?

- What do you most want in this relationship?

- What do you think this relationship wants from the two of us?

- Are you willing to address these issues?

- When do you want to start?

Who starts first could be decided by the flip of a coin. After you've taken time to honestly listen to your partner, switch roles. If it's too difficult for you to do this at this point in your relationship, or if you believe that either of you wouldn't be real or honest, then ask each other if you would be willing to spend an hour or two with a therapist, coach or spiritual guide. Whatever you do, make it as safe as possible and begin.

C. Self-esteem

Legitimacy is an image of groundedness, of belonging, of being genuinely who you are. That is your right. The idea of being an orphan conveys that you only partially access your birthright.

To help you move from acting like an orphan to claiming your legitimate place in the world we invented a little process and called it self esteem. Here's my take on one pathway to legitimacy.

Self-esteem is a couple of words we use often but rarely do we know what we mean by those words. It's a lot like the words marriage, love, patriotism or even words like good or bad. These words float in and out of our mouths without precise meaning.

To esteem your own self would mean to me that you honor your truth, that you know what you're feeling when you're feeling it and that you respect that feeling. Esteem of self would also include a great deal of spiritual self-knowledge. Low self-esteem would look like a person who has little individual spiritual knowledge but who readily parrots the latest eloquent words he or she hears.

Self-esteem would also look like psychological legitimacy – a person who has taken their wounds and losses, faced them and integrated them into their working personality in a transformative way.

To get there may be your life's work. You can start with a few simple observations. We lay it out in four steps each of which feed the following steps and all loop back on each other "driving" a process, which, in a simple way, will help you begin.

Caution: If you have sufficient information about what marriage is for, and you've taken the time to acquire competencies and skills

The Self-Esteem Cycle of Increasing Self Worth

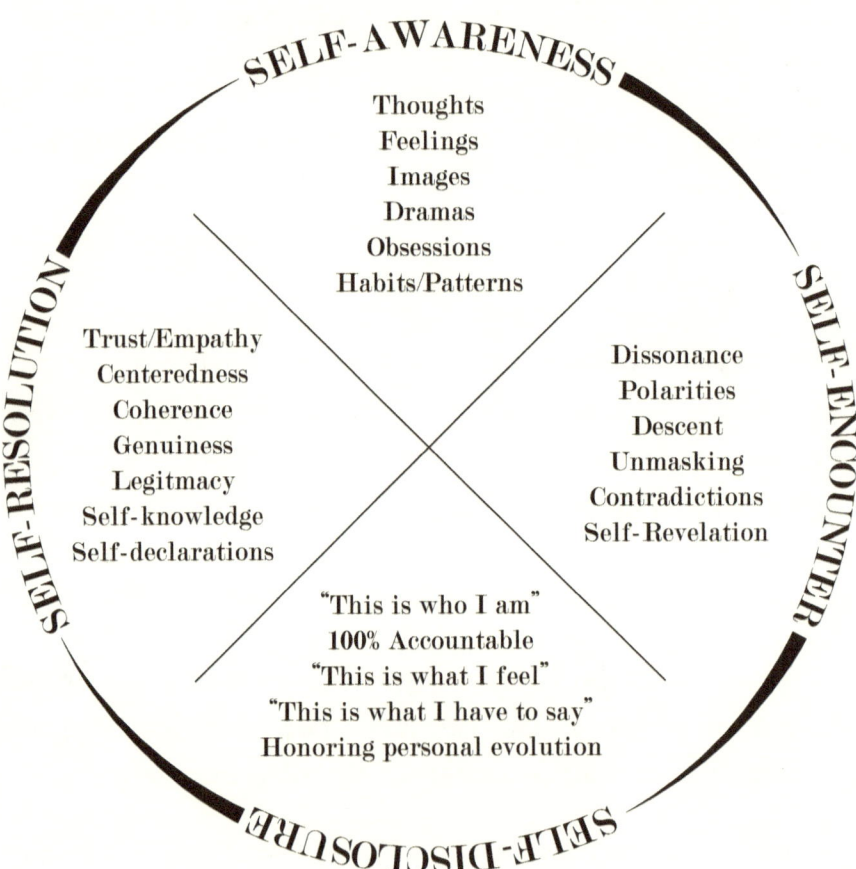

SELF-AWARENESS

Thoughts
Feelings
Images
Dramas
Obsessions
Habits/Patterns

SELF-RESOLUTION

Trust/Empathy
Centeredness
Coherence
Genuiness
Legitmacy
Self-knowledge
Self-declarations

SELF-ENCOUNTER

Dissonance
Polarities
Descent
Unmasking
Contradictions
Self-Revelation

SELF-DISCLOSURE

"This is who I am"
100% Accountable
"This is what I feel"
"This is what I have to say"
Honoring personal evolution

necessary to high functioning as a couple, and though you've created a philosophy of marriage that truly represents who you are and are now able to return regularly to your personal Garden of Eden, but lack a strong base in your own self-worth and legitimate right to love as well as be loved, your marriage will not grow. Magnificent marriages require strong leadership by both partners. And personal authority, key to loving effectively, is the ground of strong leadership.

Self-worth is not magical nor is it only for the lucky few raised in good and nurturing households. For most of us, it is not an event either or a dramatic breakthrough at a weekend retreat. Self-worth is the result of attentiveness to your world together with a willingness to "unlearn" patterns, images and well-rehearsed responses learned from others. Self-worth is a major indicator of individuality but, unfortunately, individuality is not always an indicator of self-worth.

1. Working with the Process of Self-worth

Earlier on I told you a story about the red jeep. The woman who said to me "my, how you do ramble on," was well placed in my own journey toward growing my self-worth. You might say the universe as a teacher planted her there.

My own childhood contributed to a sense of marginalization. When you're marginalized you can't change into claiming a sense of belonging simply by insight. It takes work and work builds muscle. The woman who shamed me that day became a day at the gym for me. I used what she said to look at how little I expected from others (thereby "rambling" when I was not *aware* that I was doing so). And, I took it further.

I began to pay attention to who was listening to me or taking what I had to say seriously, and who was not. I began to *encounter* realities that weren't comfortable. Once you begin, you can't stop.

Having noticed another person's response I began to share that knowledge with them. I *disclosed* what I saw happening. This, of course, created conflict but it was *conflict out where I could see it instead of the self-demeaning inner conflict I was used to walking around with.*

Notice how a sense of my own worth is building in this process. Causing trouble may be one of the best self-esteem builders we have. People around you don't necessarily want you to notice how they're relating to you or how you're relating to them. Orphans try not to notice (or dramatize what they do see). To be a grown up (strong self-worth) causes a lot of trouble if, in your life, you are surrounded by non-grown ups who choose to stay that way.

> If you think illegitimate, you'll feel illegitimate and behave as if you are illegitimate.

So, here's how the orphan would experience low self-worth. You will wander around not having any idea of how you impact others. You will have little competence to deal with their impact on you. You will drift from conversation to conversation but few will make any real difference in your life or in the life of others. You'll wonder if your existence makes any difference to anyone at all.

What got *my* attention was a bleeding ulcer. I finally admitted this to myself one day when I found myself sitting in the middle of my front lawn crying uncontrollably.

My first visit to a therapist was amazing. After telling him what I thought were my troubles, my loneliness, my frustration with my life, my empty marriage for the better part of an hour, I asked what I should "work on" between this hour and our next appointment.

He looked at me and said, "Well, you don't listen very well." I left with a ringing in my head. *I was a professional listener! How could he say that! Maybe I just had the wrong therapist. When I get home, I'll cancel our next appointment.*

Steaming mad and full of indignation, I drove straight to a friend's house. "Do you consider me a good listener?" I asked, confident of an affirmative response. He hesitated, and in that moment of hesitation, a notion I hadn't even considered before began to grow within.

"You want me to answer truthfully?" he said. "Of course I do," I insisted. "Well to be honest, no. You act like you're listening but you really seem to me to be waiting until I finish so that you can say what you want to say. I don't think you particularly care about what I'm saying."

I was floored and the recognition growing within me made me feel ashamed. I believed that I worked hard at being a listener others could trust, and yet, here two trusted people told me that they didn't consider me a good listener at all.

> Marginalizing your own presence will make it nearly impossible to listen to anyone. If you can't hear yourself, how can you hear others?

In the weeks and months following I had plenty of opportunity to confirm this revelation. For the first time in my life I was being given feedback that wasn't tailored to make me comfortable or not upset me. No wonder I had developed a bleeding ulcer. I was eating bad food in the form of lies and half-truths my entire life.

My not listening to others was directly related to low self-worth, which was related to others not listening to me. Not only was I not *aware* that I didn't listen to others, but when others tried to make me aware I avoided hearing what they had to say. Not only that but I had denied or suppressed the reality of others not listening to me. I didn't know how to work with clear, honest communication. When it did occur, I usually dismissed it and the one delivering it as having some kind of problem.

2. Claiming Your Right to Self-esteem

Legitimacy is all about *birthright*. Not the papers given to you at birth but the papers given to you by all creation on the day you were born. Legitimacy is about your core spiritual and psychological lineage, your right to be here as fully as the moon and stars.

Legitimacy means you know that you belong. You've claimed it. You've transcended your doubt, wounds and losses to create a deep connection to the eternal. Legitimacy is about a proactive stance towards your loving, your being and your truth.

Here's a story. My father was born in Switzerland. His father was an abusive alcoholic. When my father came to the United States at 15 years old he was deeply grateful for the freedoms this country offered – personal as well as political freedoms. He raised his children to be grateful for life in America as well, but he went beyond that. He would say, "We're not Swiss, we're Americans." That was well intentioned and in a big way, true. But, we were also Swiss. Somewhere in the seventh or eighth year of my therapy I decided to visit the land of my origins and go to the village where my father was born. It was the village of Gais in the canton of St. Gallen.

One afternoon, standing alone on a mountainside outside of town I decided to do a few minutes of meditation. Closing my eyes I visualized my ancestors – shepherds, farmers, caretakers of animals. As I stood there I soon heard music coming from the village below. When I opened my eyes I realized I had been in that meditative state for over an hour. I was opening to my roots and even though my ancestors were all long gone, I felt a profound right to be standing in that spot on that day, as if I lived there all my life.

Belonging, connecting with your ancestry, believing in your right to have a voice, imagining your own birthright – is the stuff of legitimacy in living.

Another aspect of legitimacy that is essential to healthy partnerships and beyond that, healthy communities, is this: If I stand firmly in the reality of my belonging – to a family, to a community, in this world – a legitimate child who is legitimately a son or daughter, who legitimately loves, feels, thinks and has presence – then I will show up as legitimate in partnership with my wife. *Only then, can I honor her legitimacy as well.* This is the psychological, spiritual and emotional basis for *empathy* for I cannot really recognize someone else's legitimacy if I'm living outside of my own.

Taken further, *if we both live within our legitimate right to be here, our conflicts will morph from power struggles (who is more legitimate?) to true empathic collaboration. Imagine the possibilities for communities, states and nations.*

Now, take this look at legitimacy and compare it to the psychological orphan. Awareness of how you orphan yourself is the first step in increasing self-worth. Orphans ignore their own alienation or blame it on others. Awareness is key to beginning to get 'your hands around' chronic feelings of loneliness, distance, low-grade anger (sometimes called hostility), the sense that you are not lovable, and continuous anxiety.

> Orphans can't be truly empathic because all wounds are self-referenced. It's all about them.

Awareness prompts (if you welcome it) *encounter*. Like this: Could it be true that my chronic tiredness is not from lack of sleep, life's pressures or bad diet? Could it be that my tiredness is indicative of my separation from my own legitimacy? Could it be that I've denied the brutality of my own distancing from others, that I've ignored the powerful needs I have, that I've indulged a diagnosis of those close to me that is useless. Useless except as a means of further alienating myself? Is my anger not about others after all?

3. Inability to Love – The Key to Loneliness

Awareness drives deeper reflection – memories, dreams, wounds and losses – long neglected, if you allow yourself to *encounter* it.

Increasing self-encounter makes us uncomfortable. Most reading this will want to skip over it because you think you've thought about it enough. You may even think there's nothing new in here for you. I ask you to indulge me with a little patience as we take this deeper.

Encountering the stuff of self-imaginings drives another need. We need to tell someone. We need to connect because the very act of encountering anger, loss, wounds and their effect on relationships is an act of legitimacy. It is as if you are saying to yourself "I have a right to work through this and I have a right to live out loud in this world. Further, I want others to know me." This is the need for *disclosure*.

So now we can begin to see the *process* of increasing self-worth. *Awareness* is stimulated perhaps by a conversation, a book, a partner or a life crisis. Taking your own inner life seriously, you begin to *encounter* the patterns you have used to avoid feelings or truth or reality. Encountering your own stuff drives a need to *disclose* who you are to others close to you. Or, perhaps you start with a therapist, coach or spiritual advisor.

> If you ask me what I came into this world to do, I will tell you. I came to live out loud.
> —Emile Zola

Encountering and disclosing begins to close the distance between you and your natural right to feel legitimate. This awareness of your right to be here, to speak, to feel, to have your own thoughts and opinions, to love in your own idiosyncratic way, to be in *this* world, at *this* time, the person you are – is the manifestation of self-worth.

You are increasing self-worth and simultaneously changing the rules by which you survived. You can change the rules because you've begun to change the paradigm that you cobbled together in the face of an unwelcoming environment.

Making your marriage sing is about facing (awareness) and exposing (encountering) the paradigm you each dragged into this marriage. Disclosing the toxic aspects of that paradigm, as well as the inadequate foundation of some of its premises is an act of increased self-worth. To build a new foundation based on your loving of each other, your own deeply held beliefs and values, your commitment to growing your marriage until "death do you part" is, perhaps, the grandest way you can express the esteem you're building.

> When we are present with one another, all opinions, theories, hypotheses, diagnoses, analyses, criticisms and other "distancers" are absent from our relationship.

If you really "got" the above you can skip this next section. For those of you who, like me, need new things said in several different ways before they soak in, here's the process laid out differently, as I see it.

4. The Self-Esteem Process

a. Self-awareness. The simple truth is we all believe we are very much aware of who we are and what we feel. And we are, somewhat. But the awareness of self that I'm talking about is probably a bit subtler than the one you're used to. The comment by my therapist that may or may not have been intended to have the impact it had on me was like a bomb going off behind my defenses. I had until then, successfully kept my listening incompetence hidden behind my cheerleading persona. Perhaps that is why I went to the therapist in the first place. Perhaps I had enough of dysfunction in my relationships, perhaps the planets were aligned just right that day – I don't know. I do know that moment of awareness ignited the need for an entire journey.

Many of us think we're aware when we're not. This is the cause of much unhappiness in marriage. One partner will say, "how can she/he not see it? It's so obvious." They'll take that little piece of awareness and extend it to a diagnosis of their partner's intentions, love and even viability as a partner.

Superiority and resignation are relationship killers. They naturally lead to criticism, which leads to defensiveness, which the researcher John Gottman calls the first two of the "four horsemen of the apocalypse" in marriage.

Fear of intimacy engenders superiority and resignation because they both keep you in your old paradigm where there's little room for and less invitation to real awareness. Not only that but superiority breeds superiority in response.

We offer the 100% rule as a pathway to break down this competitive dance. You'll both have to surrender 100% to the reality that both of you have serious work to do.

Do not confuse your individual need for learning with the fantasy that "this marriage is not going to work" or "I guess we're just incompatible."

Awareness includes thinking, feeling and imagining and they drive your mood, fuel your anger, alter your state, and seduce you into being an orphan. You use up a great deal of energy living an illusion. To change, you'll need the courage of honest self-reflection.

Tuning into your own feelings (not your diagnosis of your partner expressed as a feeling statement, e.g., "I feel you just don't love me."), would look like this, "I'm lonely and lost. I don't know how to love you and I can't find a path to being close to you."

Giving feelings space to emerge – your loneliness, for example – without attaching them to or projecting them onto another, takes discipline and art. You have to admit that while you may have once been a victim of lack of love, today, loving is your choice and your responsibility. Loving is your pathway to having the love you want.

Taking full responsibility for your thinking (beliefs, values) might look like this: "I can see that my mother's attitude towards men has strongly influenced my willingness to take risks with my partner." Or this: "Men at work tend to embrace attitudes towards women that I may not share but rarely challenge. I can see how that might affect my ability to listen to my partner."

Our imaginations are full of distortions, projections and fear-based images. Owning what I bring here could look like this: "Relationships aren't meant to last long term," "Men are naturally polygamists," "Marriage doesn't really add anything to relationships," and this, "Women just marry for the paycheck." These are examples of degraded imaginative processes that contaminate your ability to increase your self-awareness.

Here are a few phrases people have given me that they identified as critical learning in their developmental years: "Control yourself," "Be reasonable," "Mature people don't act so emotional," "Boys don't cry," "Good girls don't say things like that," "You'll upset your mother," "Father's tired, don't bother him," and so on. It would be a good exercise if you stopped here and added some of your own. These phrases were uttered out of someone's fear. Their effect on children however is devastating because they 'frame' relationship expectations. If I really believe that 'boys shouldn't cry' how can I partner with a woman who not only expects but cherishes my vulnerability?

The critical learning of fear based limitations distorts my capacity to freely relate to my honey.

Things I've learned that keep me from realizing intimacy with my partner.

_____

_____

_____

_____

_____

_____

_____

_____

_____

_____

_____

_____

_____

_____

_____

_____

_____

_____

_____

_____

_____

_____

Self-awareness cannot worry about what's appropriate, or what you *should* be thinking, or what's right and wrong. Self-awareness is simply about admitting, as truthfully as possible, what you *do* think, feel and believe.

Notice as you begin to examine your own inner territory that you'll probably feel some fear. The fear is this: if you take full responsibility for all the distortions you bring to the relationship, can you trust your partner to do the same? This is a legitimate fear. In our workshops we do a considerable amount of work around the idea of the "buy in." You'll need to risk, it's true, but it is also legitimate to expect that your partner is willing (and able) to risk as well.

Many of us come from families that have been strongly (perhaps not intentionally) influenced by a puritan-like heritage of suppression. Individual truth is not to be trusted, feelings are dangerous, behavior must be constantly modified in the name of appropriateness, politeness is a supreme value, social correctness marks you as mature and so on.

Suppression is suppression whether it's well intentioned or not. To break out of a marginal marriage and to begin singing your marriage into a joyful reality will take deep courage from both of you.

Awareness is the conscious decision to allow yourself to know yourself. It requires you to Stop! Look! and Listen! to what you are thinking, feeling and imagining at any given moment. It also requires a withdrawal from the urge to focus on what your partner is thinking, feeling or imagining. If there's trust, they will tell you.

Awareness pushes us into self-encounter.

2. Self-encounter

If you are aware of what you feel when you feel it, and are competently tuned into images you work with daily, and if you are clear about what you believe and think – then your challenge is to move from a "self-reinforcing loop" in your own isolated world into the heart of self-encounter. Awareness drives encounter if encounter is not avoided or denied.

This, perhaps, is at the heart of growth in self-worth. If you cannot link these two, there will be no change in how you relate.

I knew a man who liked to say, "Of course, I'm a jerk. I like being a jerk." He wasn't interested in encountering his style or in evaluating his impact on others. He thought it was funny to be isolated, superior and cut off even though his children and wife suffered greatly from his adolescent attitude.

I guessed that though he said he was okay with being a jerk, he hadn't yet let himself face (awareness/encounter) the personal pain behind all this, nor could he see the anger, sorrow and loneliness that his created character put on others.

Had he descended into awareness he would have to face the betrayals, wounds and losses of his tumultuous childhood. He would have to encounter how deeply hurt he was. It would take great courage for him to do so.

Encounter requires willingness – conscious and intentional. Sometimes we are lucky enough to experience a loss so great or frightening that we are able to get there. Sometimes, it's the threat of divorce; sometimes, it's losing a job or a death of someone close.

Self-encounter is at the heart of the 100% rule. It becomes a working principle for couples who want their marriage to grow. It's a very nice alternative to partner-encounter though partner-encounter is also necessary and will come, but only when self-encounter is firmly established.

Change. What you relate to as permanent and unchanging changed before you finished reading this sentence or thought that thought. Relationships thrive on energy always moving around. Relationships hate stagnation. Your changes and your willingness to face them create a space where it is easier for your partner to do the same. You might say that the successful embrace of conflict, the flagship of change, rests on your competency in self-encounter.

Self-encounter opens the way for the creative expansion of your paradigm. Incorporating new information stretches the images you bring to relationship, allows you to discard that which is no longer relevant (travel light on this journey), pushes the evolution of beliefs about relationship and deepens emotional connection.

When I was a child I thought like a child, I reasoned like a child, but when I became a grown up, I put childish ways behind me. This is to say, I fully embrace the full spectrum of my emotional authority, my psychological complexity and my spiritual depth.

Today is not only the first day of the rest of your life. In terms of your marriage, it is the only day.

Encounter opens you to the possibilities of your life today and it pushes the next natural step in expanding self-worth – the need to disclose.

3. Self Disclosure

Increasing your own awareness may have involved seeing a therapist or coach, you may have embraced conflict with your partner or a close friend and the encounter offered new information which perhaps forced you to look at some long buried feelings.

Looking inward, encountering the contours and substance of those feelings, expands your esteem by unmasking the fear, which surrounded and shielded them from you. The more you know of who you are, the greater the *possibility* of self-acceptance and the greater importance of finding a path to self-forgiveness. Acceptance is a pathway to legitimacy.

There are those who fear facing their shadow because they think it will increase self-rejection and judgment. They fear that they will feel more unacceptable than ever.

"Best to let sleeping dogs lie," an old acquaintance of mine said. I said I like my dogs awake.

There's grace in facing reality as clearly and straightforwardly as possible. We're all flawed. All of us walk with a limp. We all have reasons to feel bad about mistakes we've made. There've been betrayals, shadowy half-truths and lapses. All of us have come up short when our fullest attention was required. None of us have loved to our capability. Distance, judgment, coldness, rejection are familiar to all of us.

Encounter is a pathway to the grace of ending your own isolation. It is an invitation to accept yourself – whether you like it or not, you are human. Just like the rest of us.

But you cannot live in a naive kind of self-encounter, absorbed with yourself, referencing all input to yourself or obsessed with your own wounds. Narcissism is always a possibility in self-encounter. The next naturally occurring step in increasing self-worth is the need for self-disclosure.

Healthy self-disclosure is an act of intimacy and a pathway itself into deep relationship. It is an act of love as well. It moves you from the island created to keep you safe towards the shore of belonging.

Revealing, exposing and disclosing the discoveries you're making expands as you commit to *this* marriage, at *this* time in *this* place. I often find that when I sit down to talk with my honey over some (inner) work I've been doing, that the disclosure itself provokes further self-encounter. Awareness drives encounter, which is fed by the need for disclosure which fuels further awareness and opens to further encounter.

> In the heat of our relationship we are both straining to become all that we can be.

We choose relationships with the ones we chose because we are driven to move deeper into self-definition beyond the comfort zone we were in when we married and beyond what we knew of our own loving.

"It is to be broken; it is never whole."

4. Self Resolution

The amazing thing about marriages that sing is they are like rivers – they never stop flowing. Change is a friend, always present. Heraclitus said long ago, "The only thing that doesn't change, is change itself."

Marriages that sing embrace change, have the capacity to see change as opportunity, and live in anticipation of what's next. The river flows, there are rocks, high spots, low spots, bends and eddies – and the river flows. Storms come, drought happens, yet the river keeps flowing…

Change and coming to terms with the way each of us is, as our relationship is, evolving requires many small course corrections. Each growth spurt, each new way of seeing, each challenge integrated as a shift in expectations – all rely on our coming together in understanding.

You could say it this way: Awareness drives encounter, which forces the need for disclosure. Disclosure is often accompanied by dissonance. We'll somehow have to come to terms with this next new thing if we are to be genuinely coupled. And we'll have to integrate the new thing in a way that expands the marriage conversation. We may even celebrate our metamorphosis as we marvel at the new green shoots of our learning.

Resolution is not about ending, it's about the creation of a new piece in the ever-evolving structure of our marriage. Here's an example.

For years he told his wife how much he liked tuna fish sandwiches. He was a fireman and working full shifts, she packed his food in a cooler he could access as needed. She always made a tuna fish sandwich regardless of what else she put in there.

One morning as he was getting ready to leave he said to her, "Could you make me something different than tuna fish?" "I thought you liked tuna fish," she said, a little unsettled and just a little hurt. "I do, did, but I'm kind of sick of them."

Not really much of a conflict unless, of course, you factor in that he wasn't the type of guy to stay current with his feelings, who imagined that she could read his subtlest clues and she was an obsessive pleaser. That morning's conversation morphed into a larger discussion about how little they really knew about one another.

Their marriage ended in divorce. Not because of the tuna fish sandwich but because it was an accurate indicator of the deep abyss between them and their almost adolescent inability to communicate.

Resolution would have taken an entirely different direction than divorce. A healthy couple perhaps would have a good laugh. Or maybe she'd put a tuna fish sandwich under his pillow. He might have used the occasion to tell her some other feelings he held back and they might have achieved a new understanding, opening communication that needed to be opened.

Resolution would then look like a small milestone in their continuing commitment to understand, reveal and challenge and so grow their intimacy.

Resolution leads to more awareness. If they can see and address the "tuna fish phenomenon" they can use it to provoke awareness in other situations where open communication is difficult for them.

Resolution provokes encounter. Should they be able to laugh at the tuna fish thing, each of them will no doubt do some work on how they individually dumb down good communication.

Notice the cascading effects as each component of self-worth stimulates and provokes the next, always looping around, keeping the cycle of awareness > encounter > disclosure > resolution > awareness/encounter going – if you focus on it, if you insist on it.

Without a commitment to increasing your competency in honoring who you are you cannot get to the gift you bring into relationship. Your own natural genius, a critical relationship factor, needs for its manifestation honoring of your feelings, thoughts, images and deepest spiritual instincts and beliefs.

Your unique gift, your irrevocable place in the family of humans is the reason you were chosen to be in this relationship by the person who chose you.

D. Natural Genius: The Gold Hidden in the Dust

Ever ask: What am I here for? What is this life all about? Ever wonder about your own obituary?

"Here lies Sam Smith. He died at seventy-one years old. He mowed a good lawn. His car was always clean. Sam occasionally ate too many French fries. He liked TV, he was faithful to his wife, you never heard Sam raise his voice. We'll miss Sam, that is, if we can remember him."

Your individual *gift* is what we want to talk about now. Most of us don't linger here because we erroneously think our failures are our most important legacy. Perhaps we aren't as much like other people as we thought we should be.

I heard a sermon once that picked this up. The pastor's theme was "Jesus the oddball." He invited the audience to re-imagine all they knew about Jesus. He said some far out things. "Imagine a guy who never showered, never brushed his teeth, never changed his underwear," he began. He had our attention.

"Imagine a regular day laborer, a carpenter's helper maybe, who hung out and drank beer with the local low lifes," he went on. "He left his family, had no church connections, no education and wasn't politically astute. He was unemployed, wandered from town to town, ignored local customs and thought he represented God."

Then the pastor leaned forward and fairly shouted "Who was this guy?"

As he developed his theme he artfully transformed it into taking a look at our own passivity, our own adaptability and our fear of standing out. He said things like "Christianity is about fully manifesting your own potential, it's about taking power away from social structures and attitudes that kill human uniqueness, and it's about living without fear."

That's what he said, and much more. I walked out thinking about my own gifts. What did I bring into the world that didn't show up in the way my lawn was mowed or my checkbook was balanced? Was there something unique about me that I hadn't yet discovered?

Each of us brings a gift into the world that, when discovered and offered to the world makes it better. That's a revolutionary idea. I started thinking that the answer was yes. I read James Hillman's *The Soul's Code* and a few other books that point that way.

Then this. If we each bring a gift into this world, it is also true that the world, in a sense, depends on us discovering and offering that gift in order for the world to thrive. One way we could do that is to find it and offer it within our own marriage.

Perhaps divorce happens, or numbness happens, or chronic arguments happen, when neither individual in a marriage is able to identify what their own and then, what their partner's natural genius is. Without knowing and honoring this gift, all communication becomes linear. Conversation becomes conversation about today's news, roommate challenges, and, perhaps, choice of entertainment.

Later on we'll introduce you to the CAPPS model for serious communication. The first component of CAPPS is curiosity. Couples who are floundering have lost their ability to be curious about their partners. They live with their assumptions about who their partner is. Curiosity is a hugely necessary competence in discovering your partner's natural genius. It is also necessary for sustainable intimacy.

One reason that lifelong commitment is so vitally a part of marriage is that identifying and developing and standing up for your own gift is a lifelong challenge. It is also another pathway to claiming your legitimacy. If you can realize your gift then you may be able to recognize your partner's gift as well. You'll experience the beginnings of true empathy. You'll also naturally become increasingly curious about who this genius is that you chose to spend your life with. Your arguments will look a lot different to both of you as you leave the competitive power-based dance we're all familiar with, and move into discovery, exploration, revelation and intimate talk.

Notice. We are not at all going into gender differences here. What a woman brings to partnership because of her unique orientation and gifts as a woman and what a man brings because of his gifts and the way he is hard wired have received a lot of attention.

We choose to stay with individual genius as a contribution to relational vitality.

It's really not surprising that many marriages end in divorce. They are mostly still trying to liberate themselves from early adolescent fears and fantasies. This liberation quest, though natural, does not deserve to be projected onto your partner.

Legitimacy is a gift of the universe. Natural genius is a natural conse-quence of finding your legitimacy. Once discovered you'll begin to see why so many arguments are really useless power struggles that keep both partners in self-chosen misery.

If you follow this, I'll show you something else. If you cannot follow this, email me and I'll help you. Here's why I like this model so much and why I believe that if you embrace it, you can sing your marriage into celebration.

Remember the **Seven Principles** – a philosophy of marriage. In there is the "need to be seen." This need, I said, is clearly apparent in children but we never grow out of it. Each of us wants to be seen not so much for what we *do* (although that's nice, too) but for who we *are*.

We want our partner to know that we know something special. That we understand what everyone around us is talking about and that we have a little different point of view. If our partner is tuned into who we are – our natural, idiosyncratic, unique, unusual, annoying and distinct perspective – and we are tuned in to them, we can have a lot of fun.

Mass culture influences us but doesn't satisfy us. It never can. It can't because its premise is that we are all alike. It can, by definition, never see the individuals it is pitching. A mass culture approach to relationship will not work either.

We not only want to *be seen*, we want to *see* those we love. Communication depends on listening competencies and listening depends on seeing. Hearing the words only of those you love and giving words back doesn't qualify as communication – unless, of course, you're only asking for the time of day.

Seeing and listening are inextricably wound around natural genius in this way. When you begin to get a sense of your own uniqueness and when you begin to sense the individual uniqueness of your partner you have a different inner context for imagining them even as you listen to them. If I know my partner uniquely observes around and about the powerless beings of the world – children, outcasts, the lonely, those on the lowest tier of power, spiders and ants – then what she says will be heard by me in the context of what I know about her.

I once entertained the CEO of a company I consulted for, at my home. One morning he came out of the guest bathroom agitated about a spider in the shower. I said, "I hope you didn't hurt it." He looked at me as if I just told him to take a bath in yogurt. "You need to kill those things!" he ordered.

I said, "You don't understand. My wife will take that spider out of the shower on a piece of tissue and put it back outside. We don't use poisons around here and she won't have anyone killing spiders." His eyes widened, "She must be crazy," he said.

My partner's craziness is part of her deeper natural genius. She sees the helpless and powerless more clearly than almost anyone I know. She naturally protects and cares for them whether animal or human.

I believe the world is a better place because she does this, and seeing that she does this opens my eyes to other attitudes she brings to our relationship that I might otherwise miss.

The pathway. You getting to know you takes focus, attentiveness and deep curiosity. I think of it as a kind of descent out of the buzzing, swirling everyday world of activity, demands and distractions. You'll need the help of friends. You may want the help of a professional coach or therapist. You'll certainly want to invite your partner into the conversation if your relationship is healthy enough to sustain this journey.

We ask people, in a small group, to focus on the times in their lives when they absolutely knew they made an impact on someone else. Then we ask them to tell the story. Others observe what is special or unique about the occurrence. They look for an unusual point of view, or an unusual problem solving strategy. They'll inquire about feelings and attitudes in the story, also about what happened *after* the story ends. The story will open dialogue, exploration, reflection and revelation and soon the storyteller begins to get a sense of what they brought to that situation that stands out, what happened that was extraordinary. This then can become a platform, albeit a small one, to build the discovery of personal uniqueness upon.

Most of us need a light to guide us as the stars guided seafarers for hundreds of years before modern navigational instruments were invented. Initially your light – a friend, partner or coach – will point out things about you that are hard for you to see. You may think it arrogant to notice your own genius, or you may dismiss it as contrived. But if you stay with it, in faith, soon the light of your natural genius becomes an inner light and you'll find yourself standing up for what you uniquely see without compromise or apology.

A man in a workshop gave us this image. "I felt like I left this world, this time. I began to see images of myself that I had never seen before. I was a baby in a manger surrounded by animals even the smells of a barn drifted in. Clearly I went to another place, a place of birth and I saw a light shine on me as if illuminating me from the inside out."

Later he talked of a history of stuttering, of always feeling like the odd kid and family members trying to shame him out of his speech impediment. This man was a physicist. His relational gift showed up as one of incredible ability to see through both his own and his partner's challenges without drama or anxiety.

To get to your own natural genius will take a place of simplicity and safety, a "manger" where no one is observing for fame or fortune. It's a place easily passed by and will not be listed on your resume.

Finding your natural genius, the truly unusual child within, is not at all like degrees or promotions. There will be no "news at six" to celebrate your discovery. Emerging from that world and into this world will take a strong belief in your own legitimacy.

What might it look like when you've finally touched the reality of your gift? Here are a few observations given to us following a workshop on natural genius.

"I've never felt so peaceful. I could feel myself deciding to go with a sort of hunch, kind of like I was protecting a secret. One day walking in Westwood and looking in the windows of shops I let go of my criticisms of fashion and that day I knew my own designs were unique and valuable." (Kristy is a designer of women's clothes).

"In therapy I was encouraged to work hard on my dreams. I resented it because it disturbed my sleep to do so, then I started to need less sleep and I seemed to have more energy during the day. Working on my own 'genius' took something off my shoulders, a weight and I felt lighter. I began to draw as I often did when I was a child, scenes of buildings collapsing involving me somehow and the colors, ambience and tone of these scenes. My life is changing though I'm not sure where it will go. Late one night as I stood in my usually noisy but now quiet front yard, one star seemed to be winking at me. I know about visual tricks, but this was impressive and I closed my eyesto see what I'd see. I stood there alone for fifteen or twenty minutes it seemed and when I opened my eyes the sun was coming up.

"The next night I had a dream of an elegantly dressed lady guiding me down a path, which became a tunnel. We came into a clearing, a cave-like place. There were warriors there dressed in something like ancient costumes perhaps South American. They were expecting me and together we walked deeper into the cave where we met their spokesperson who handed me a finely carved spear dressed with amazingly beautifulfeathers and colors and bits of leather. The spokesperson took a string of pearls from his pocket and placed them around my neck." (Soon after this Tony enrolled in a prestigious art school quitting his job as an office manager.)

Who we are, the gift we bring, is more often than not, not obvious to us. Claiming it, an act of self-worth, opens to a demand that we honor it. Honoring it will undoubtedly change your life.

Increasingly increasing self-worth, honoring your natural genius and believing in your own legitimacy will ground you as you challenge your relationship to be all it can be. You'll have to challenge each other as well to "buy in" to a process of getting to the unknown and difficult conversations. You'll have to unmask the sacred cows that you've kept off limits and you'll have to honor each other's doofusness as you stumble around finding a path to celebration.

> We offer email coaching for those who need it and we have other resources available on our website – www.marriageconversation.com. Your job is to reach for the song that has been there for you, waiting to be sung out loud.

E. Discipline

What does it take to show up in relationship *as if* you love, *as if* you are eager to realize your full potential in this marriage and are willing to give it your all? What focus will you bring to the challenge of moving your marriage into magnificence, treating it as a precious resource and your love as your integrity?

We know that there's an art to loving. We know, too, that we can all lose focus. Life swirls around us tempting us with its many distractions. To increase the odds of "staying in the game" we'll need to understand and embrace four attitudes we bring into relationship. We call them disciplines because discipline conveys an attitude of focus, continuity, purpose and intention.

These four feed relationship excellence: physical discipline, spiritual discipline, psychological discipline and emotional discipline.

1. Physical Discipline

If I eat fast foods, drink every night, smoke, get little or no exercise, never stretch my muscles, indulge in sweets – the chances of my body working well are slim to none.

Whether you are considering quiet conversations in the evenings, playful sex, taking on a challenge through embracing conflict, or the ecstasy of lovemaking, you need physical strength and stamina to maximize the possibilities of intimacy. Notice the word stamina – it comes from stamen and brings a sense of root or core strength.

Tired, undernourished, poorly exercised bodies can't support vital loving. What they do support is moodiness, distance, anger and blame as you both work too hard against your body's lack of vitality.

What's behind our cavalier attitude towards our own health? How is it we are given these miraculous bodies and that we take them for granted? Why are we not able to connect the dots between how we treat our bodies and what we expect from them? I know people who are more mindful of the bedroom needing to be painted then they are of their bodies needing exercise.

Here are a few thoughts on why many of us disregard our body's basic health needs.

A consistent heavy demand on our schedules fools us into shaping our priorities so that care of our bodies comes last. I say "fools us" because many of the things on our schedule can be combined with smart body care. For example, a supermarket is about five blocks from our home. I can jump in the car, ride my bike or walk. If I'm fixated on time, I'll drive. If I'm tuned into my body, I'll walk.

The availability of food that is less than healthy and is served quickly is another trick on the way to less than vibrant health. I'll justify it because I'm rushed. The illusion of "not enough time" will trick me into a bad decision, and my body will lose.

What about time? The "not enough time" illusion is a powerful one. I discovered some years ago several successful people who were not only physically fit, but seemed blessed with an abundance of time. One, a CEO I'll call Jeff, had an open door policy at work. Executives, managers and regular workers in the plant could come by at almost anytime and he'd be available.

One day I asked him how he did that. He said, "I never procrastinate on any task. I take care of everything I can as quickly as possible. There are no stacks of unfinished business on my desk. If my children call I take the call and spend time with them right there. If I can't do that I'll call back immediately following that which was taking my attention.

I rise at four thirty a.m. and work out for an hour and a half. I spend the hour after showering in meditation and prayer. My family and I share breakfast and I'm at the office by eight thirty. We don't watch television in the evenings for the most part, and spend time with each other and on family projects. We are a disciplined family and we reap great rewards for our focus."

You'll notice Jeff speaks as if energy isn't a challenge. He takes care of his body. So does his family. Tasks delayed are an energy drainer. He sees to it that that doesn't happen. Family dramas expand if they are avoided. Jeff works hard to stay current in his relationships. He believes in being present in the present.

He is able to see through the illusions of "not enough time" and instead co-created a life where priorities are clear and commitment to health is paramount.

In the words of this model of marriage, I would say that Jeff had long ago accessed his legitimacy, operated from a strong sense of self-worth and wasn't afraid to lead.

One day he told me that his family always parked far away from a supermarket or mall entrance. They enjoyed a brisk walk, never worried about parking, and their well-maintained car wasn't all dinged up from doors opened in tight places.

Healthy families are a lot alike in that they embrace life – they look for new ways to enjoy each other and are forever curious about opportunities for learning.

Awareness of your body and its needs comes first. Encountering the truths of how you related to your physical vitality follows. Inviting a consciousness partner (the need for disclosure) seals the process. Accountability, feedback and resolve (see above on the fourth step of increasing self-worth), by setting benchmarks of health, carry the process along.

2. Emotional Life Discipline

Hormones didn't carry us far. We discovered, overnight it seemed, that real challenges awaited and the partner we chose and so loved was far more complex that we realized. We may have also realized that we were not so simple to love either. Some of us lost hope. Some divorced. Many went towards resignation and a kind of safe numbness.

A couple came to me for coaching recently and warned me on the phone that they were tough. They meant that they had already done a lot of work on their marriage and that nothing seemed to help. Their last therapist fired them.

They were both therapists themselves. Middle-aged, very bright and very successful, they said their marriage was "on hold" and very close to dissolving altogether. Theirs was a "high performance" marriage, their lives – interesting, challenging and demanding – sucked up a lot of emotional energy and there was little available for their marriage.

Nevertheless, there was desire and love and they wanted to see if they could find a path back to cherishing one another. We began with emotional incompetence.hough they were both well versed in psychological strategies for uncovering feelings, they habitually denied their feelings using shop worn excuses like "she wouldn't listen anyway," or "he's too self-absorbed to take me seriously."

He intimidated her by escalating the emotion of the moment without addressing his own vulnerability and she tried to control the escalation by tuning out and turning away. This dance lowered their emotional I.Q. and, naturally, they felt something close to shame. They knew their encounters were dishonest but they couldn't own their own contribution.

They could not grant legitimacy to their marriage or its needs either. Their incompetency repeatedly led them down emotional cul-de-sacs. Their profession and education were, in a sense, in their way because pride drove their power struggle and shame their denial of what was really needed.

We all need to descend from the airy world of intellect, conceptual thinking, logic and reason into the not so neat world of feelings – what Yeats called "the rag and bone shop of the heart."

Discipline here is not the discipline of intellect but the discipline of courage. It is the decision to descend, so to speak, to the reality of what is, rather than live in the fantasy of what ought to be.

Emotional discipline involves taking risks. I embrace awareness not of what my partner is doing/saying /feeling but of what I'm feeling *beneath* the feeling I'm talking about. Does that sound a little like gobbledygook? Here's what I mean. You may think that you're angry with your partner for coming home late but beneath that anger (which itself usually shows up as anxiety but gets ramped up into what I think of as pseudo anger) there is probably fear. The fear could be for his or her safety, or for your own possible abandonment, or even for a lack of sensitivity to you, or of many other things. The important thing is to descend to the fear and identify it.

If you do, you'll be able to communicate honestly and with courage. If you don't you very well may convert the fear into an attack (fight or flight when afraid) and that attack will distance you from the person you love. You can consider that choosing to face your fear is emotional discipline because you're not giving into the feeling that at that moment is on the tip of your tongue.

In corporate consulting, I often come across concerns about sexual harassment. Here's how that looks when talking about emotional discipline. A man (over 90% of sexual harassment cases originate with a complaint from a woman about a man) is attracted to a woman. He has long been socialized to give her all power of consent and to act like a hunter when in the grips of attraction.

His emotional I.Q. will tend to be low in this situation. He (naturally, I think, given his history) becomes anxious. He has dumbed down his natural grace and confidence, has little reliable information about his body as it relates to women, has been immersed in cultural models of charged sexual images and is probably ignorant of his own legitimacy. He doesn't know that his anxiety equals fear plus loneliness. He lacks communication skills that would ease the situation for him and for her, and he blurts out an inappropriate remark. It will take discipline for this man to recognize his fear/attraction, and to work with it without burdening the object of his attraction with his own (inner) work.

We can purposely raise our emotional I.Q. through attentiveness (awareness), self-encounter and disclosure (coaching), resolving the repetitive dramas by gaining an appreciation of the legitimacy of our feelings, and reframing the experience of anxiety.

3. Psychological Discipline

Our "post psychological" age offers some delicious ideas for self-realization and the discipline of being psychologically adept. Standing in line at your favorite coffee shop or grocery store you can hear surprising conversations that are psychologically smart.

Sometimes though, a little information is more dangerous than none at all. Without the discipline of focusing on your own psychological terrain anyone can use pieces of insight to dissect, diagnose, analyze and psychologically disembowel their partner. This is a cause of much grief in marriage.

Psychological discipline begins at home – I mean, home of origin. You'll need to do some work. For example, if I know that my mother's deep losses were put on me, her youngest son, in a way that entrapped me, and if I know that my father wasn't competent to confront her or love her in a psychologically conscious way, and if I can see the metamorphosis of those patterns as they seep into my marriage – then I may be capable of using that information to alert myself to my own blind spots.

If not that, I'll be at risk of projecting my relational incompetency onto my partner. She might even "become" my mother in my anguish and I might very well reenact my father's lack of competence.

If I am married to someone who has been adopted, and if I appreciate the depth of that experience, and if she tells me she walks around with the fear of abandonment, I will have the opportunity to be empathic. I'll need discipline however to hold this space in our relationship.

If I'm not disciplined, much of what I know can be used in analyzing her. Perhaps I'll create theories about my marriage with her as the villain, perhaps I'll look elsewhere for someone who can love me. I will not be able to understand and relate to her because I've focused on what I'm missing (in her).

Standing Under – Looking for a New Perspective, Understanding

Psychological discipline means I seek to understand, not analyze my partner. I am open to hearing her creative instinct, her history of wounds and losses, her childhood stories, her fantasies, her complaints about her own doofusness – without using any of it as ammunition for diagnosis or analysis.

My legitimacy in loving the woman I chose to be my partner is dependent on my working to realize some discipline in the care of my body, in attentiveness to my emotions and in developing an appreciation for the psychological richness I bring to this marriage.

All of this is about the health of your marriage. I like to imagine that underneath these three disciplines however, lies a fourth, which brings the juice of cosmic connection to your loving one another.

4. Spiritual Discipline

Dennis Merritt Jones in his positively hopeful book, *The Art of Being*, talks about the many names he uses for God – Source, The Infinite One, Being, Presence, Self, The Whole, Divine Mind, Life, Spirit, Universal Intelligence...

He says this: "In my mind there is one God which is known by many different names." (Introduction, *The Art of Being*, Penguin, used by permission of the author).

It took me a very long time – five undergraduate years that were laced with theology and church history and three graduate years devoted solely to the study of theology – to face that there's a very real difference between religious expertise and language, and the reality of spiritual depth. The awakening was painful and required facing my own arrogance.

"One God known by many names" translates into a potential paradigm shift for many of us. For spirituality is not about rules or theories, buildings or doctrines. Spirituality is about your willingness to expand your connection to the very ground of all life. It is not about morality but about deeply held values that are cosmically authentic and universally based, true for all men and women everywhere.

To compartmentalize spirituality and cast it in the language of a club or group misuses our very human instinct towards humility, awe and reverence. "Our hearts are restless," Pascal said, "until they find their rest in thee." Deep within there is a longing for legitimacy, belonging and the experience of deep and universal values – all of which can be misused by those whose interest is personal power and whose operating style is fear-based, controlling and essentially frightening.

Within marriage rules breed superiority. Theories breed diagnosis. If we cannot accept that we long to be grounded in the impulse to life found in all creation we will have trouble seeing our partner as an evolving, needy, loving, creative spiritual being. We will be tempted to see them through the distancing spectacles of analysis.

One hundred and fifty years ago, Soren Kierkegaard, a Danish philosopher and theologian put it this way, "Many people reach their conclusions about life like schoolboys. They cheat their master by copying the answer out of a book without having worked out the sum for themselves."

Spiritual depth and the discipline it takes to go there begin with exploring what you knew about your own beliefs and values before others tried to teach you theirs. It is a pathway of discovery and humility.

Spirit takes you toward listening to the resonance within that you may have ignored. Listening to your own resonance and that of others, especially your partner, opens the possibility of listening to the source of all resonance.

Our birth is but a sleep and a forgetting:

the soul that rises in us, our life's star,

has elsewhere its setting,

and cometh from afar:

Not in entire forgetfulness

and not in utter nakedness.

But trailing clouds of glory do we come

from God, who is our home.

Heaven lies about us in our infancy!

William Wordsworth, "Ode to Intimations of Immortality"

Knowing something of your partner's spiritual life, their responsiveness to deeply held inner values, their quickening (to use an old but poignant word) in opening to resonant awareness – awe in the presence of revelation, delight in energy of children, humility in sensing the creative process, grief in the realization of mortality – these can shape the potential for intimacy and move us from self absorption to gratitude.

These disciplines will develop your capacity for opening up channels, deep waterways, for intimate relating.

We've looked at a brief strategy for increasing self-worth and followed it with the disciplines it takes to honor your own partnership. These are not meant to be conclusive but to engage you in a different kind of conversation about your marriage – one in which you honor your own and your partner's legitimate right to love, to be seen, to change and to grow.

All of this needs a grounding competency, and that is the need to listen.

F. Listening with Purpose

Listening may well be the most reliable aphrodisiac known to man. It is a well-known fact that many of us overestimate how well we listen and underestimate our partner's ability to listen.

Listening is not simply keeping quiet, though sometimes that's a good thing. A couple I know had a bad habit of interrupting one another. Together we invented hand signals to help them stop this destructive habit. Getting a handle on the habit opened the door to new learning about listening.

Listening takes humility. It takes a kind of suspension of the certainty that comes with intimacy – the certainty is that you think you know who your partner is. The reality is we know a whole lot less than we think we know. Please repeat: *We know a whole lot less of who our partner really is than we think we know.* Even when you think you know who they are, listening to them is a central challenge of marriage.

My Uncle Fritz was a top chef at the famous Waldorf Astoria Hotel in New York City. He and my Aunt Frieda lived on Long Island and each year we were invited to go there during the holidays. Aunt Frieda would cook a roast and Uncle Fritz would create all sorts of wonderful desserts. After dinner they'd serve coffee with a huge dollop of real whipped cream on the top. I relished those trips for the banquet they provided, but I also loved Aunt Frieda and Uncle Fritz.

Uncle Fritz was physically fit and proud of it. He was handsome and lean with a fine thin mustache. Aunt Frieda always smelled delicious – those are the memory snapshots of a young boy.

One holiday season, my father gathered us in the kitchen and told us we wouldn't be going to Long Island that year. "Uncle Fritz passed away yesterday."

Here's what happened. It was early winter and he and Frieda noticed some water in one of the upstairs rooms. The roof was leaking. Uncle Fritz decided he would go up on the slate roof and repair it before it did serious damage. Aunt Frieda asked him not to do it – to wait and have a roof repairman come the next day. Uncle Fritz insisted that he'd be fine and went anyway.

Dressed as he always was in dress pants, white shirt and tie and dress shoes, he hauled out an extension ladder and put it against the side of the house. As he began climbing towards the roof, a light rain began to fall. His dress shoes were not made for this kind of activity but he went on ahead. When he got to the roof he stepped on a wet slate that had loosened in a previous storm. He slipped and fell to his death.

Uncle Fritz was, as we are, Swiss German. The men in our family do not have a history of listening to women. They lived in an old world paradigm. My father's dismissal of my mother's input was similar to Uncle Fritz's response to Aunt Frieda. The slow dismantling of that attitude has been a big part of my life's work. The work is still in progress. Listening takes courage, patience, belief and consciousness. It takes the willingness to hear another's point of view even when that point of view doesn't match any of your own beliefs. Listening can save your life.

It helps us to imagine that there are different kinds of listening because life throws different listening challenges at us each day. We've separated them (somewhat artificially) into three types for teaching purposes.

1. Active Listening

The teenage girl glared at her mother as she hissed through clenched teeth, "You have no idea who I am. You think you know me but you don't. You don't listen. All you do is talk at me. I hate your pompous lectures. I hate your religion. I hate the way you patronize dad. But most of all I hate that you pretend to know me when you don't know me at all."

Her mother, enveloped in her own worldview, was cocooned and unavailable to her daughter. She might have begun changing the gridlock between them by simply agreeing – "perhaps that's right" – and then asking her daughter to tell her who she was.

Perhaps the most commonly talked about kind of listening is the need to listen actively. Psychotherapists and business consultants teach it as a means to clarifying important communication exchanges. You would think all listening would be active but experience tells us otherwise.

Many people fake it. You know it when they do. They may have good eye contact, they may be able to repeat verbatim what you said, but something in your animal instinctual self says, "They haven't heard what I meant."

If Uncle Fritz had been actively listened to Aunt Frieda, he might have said something like this: "You're worried about my going up on the roof, aren't you? You don't think it's safe. You're afraid I'll get hurt. And, you think, in any case, it can wait until tomorrow." He might then have considered her input and taken her love for him seriously.

Instead, he probably simply waited for her to finish, dismissed her input as coming from a woman, and went on in a kind of locked in way, to his own destiny. You might say that as good of a companion that he was to my aunt he wasn't able at that moment to be a partner.

Many chronic arguments sound like this:

> "You're not listening to me!"

> "Yes I am. I just don't agree with you."

> "No you're not. You have that look that tells me you're just patronizing me."

Do you think Aunt Frieda knew Uncle Fritz had tuned her out?

Here's what it takes to listen actively and accurately. *First,* you have to give up your agenda. This means that what you think should happen, probably will not happen. What you want to be the natural conclusion to the discussion will probably turn out different than you imagined. Your idea of your partner's point of view is probably not accurate. And, frequently, an entirely new perspective will emerge that neither of you anticipated.

"I have no idea of who you are, what you're about to say, and little knowledge of the strong feelings you bring to this discussion."

Listening actively means you work to pay attention to what is being said rather than what you're afraid might be said.

The *next step* is to inquire and clarify. "Is this what you're saying?" Active listening is different from passive listening in that you are actively engaged in "getting" what your partner is saying and feeding it back as accurately as you can. There is no room for editorializing or theorizing.

All you want to do is ensure that you understand as fully as possible what is being said.

Following clarification and inquiry, you'll ask "Do I understand everything you wanted me to get?"

When your partner is confident that they been heard, it will be your turn to respond. Same rules apply.

Some people object that listening in this way takes all spontaneity out of a simple conversation. Actually it does. Active listening is an exercise used to build a discipline around respectful and accurate listening. If you learn it, listening will soon come naturally and will not seem stilted at all.

Active listening offers a standard by which to measure your listening skills. As long as you are working to increase your listening competence agreeing with each other is not important. Hearing accurately is.

We like to think there's a step down from active listening, less intense, and valid in its own right. We call this conversational listening.

2. Conversational Listening

Those of you who are tuned into the three journeys in marriage will quickly see that conversational listening is largely the language of the first journey, roommates, or the outer journey. There's a great deal of conversation in this domain much of which is not critical to the quality of the relationship. It's not exactly the red jeep conversation, but it is a kind of freewheeling sharing of observations and opinions that healthy people indulge while doing other things.

Conversational listening includes the news, the latest gossip, to-do lists, what the kids are up to, thoughts on the backyard redesign and so on. The tone is light. The information may or may not be important but that gets sorted out in time.

Conversational listening takes second place to other activities. A friend may call in midsentence, a child might need attention, or you may heed nature's call. Sometimes it's frustrating because your partner is preoccupied with other things or is immersed in their own (inner) journey.

Unfinished business – conflict that's been avoided, past wounds wanting attention, vision longing to be birthed, personal breakthroughs – can frustrate this kind of conversation if not attended to. So, in order for conversational listening to flow as it ought, you'll both need to be current in the expression of your truest needs.

Perhaps Uncle Fritz thought Aunt Frieda was "just talking" and not serious about her concern. It happens.

Remember Tevia's conversation with Golda in *Fiddler on the Roof?* He asks if she loves him, and she, in conversational mode, doesn't really get where he's going. "Golda, do you love me?" "What are you asking me that for?" she replies. "I'm married to you aren't I?" She's in conversation mode, he's in another mode we'll call resonant listening mode.

His insistence takes them both out of conversation and into intimacy – "Well, I suppose I do," she says. Then, the piece that's so very good, he says in response, "And, I suppose I love you, too."

> "It doesn't mean a thing but after 25 years, it's nice to know."

If you use the three journeys model you'll benefit from noticing where you are in any conversation. It might look like this:

"Golda, do you love me?"

Golda: "I'm folding the laundry."

Tevia: "I need to talk about our love. When can we do that?"

Golda: (pausing and considering his invitation) "Well, we could do that now, I suppose."

Tevia: "Golda, we've shared a lot of troubles together and we're no longer young. I love you, Golda."

Golda: "You're a gift, Tevia. I love you, too."

Sometimes I sit on a stool while my wife is preparing dinner. You have to understand that she is preparing dinner and fully owns the process so my watching is okay. She'll take calls from sons and daughters-in-law, friends, neighbors and colleagues. We have an eleven-year-old daughter and it's not uncommon to have two or three grandchildren present as well. Mostly they all orbit around my honey and that's the way she likes it.

If I'm bold enough (or dumb enough) to think that we might have a conversation under these conditions, I will have to be aware of where we are – clearly roommate city. If I know this, I'll lower my expectations for meaningful or serious talk. I will not try to get a decision on any matter of importance beyond "are you having wine with dinner?"

I'll let go of control, and focus on going with the flow of life as it shows up around our house at dinnertime. There will be unfinished sentences, half-baked thoughts, funky humor, partial observations – tantalizing to follow but, not now.

Those of us who want our marriages to sing the great arias of love, who want to hear John Phillip Sousa marches following a Saturday lunch, who long to rock with our honeys and sing the blues on an early foggy morning at the beach – we need the capacity and competency of resonance, the sensitivity to leave the clock, the schedule, the budget behind and to dance into the ballroom of our deep connectivity.

A third kind of listening gets us to the journey of intimate connecting:

3. Resonant Listening

Spirituality depends on resonance. Whether you're listening to the still small voice of God or your reverence is focused on opening your heart to the presence of a child, you are dependent for deep connection on the music of the cosmos.

Our left-brain dominance won't admit it but there's more life beyond the boundaries of our senses than is contained in their most rigorous observations. Resonance takes us from dance classes into the streets of Brazil. It notices the vibrations of feelings, the tremors of belief. Resonance is the tuning fork after the note is harmonized with the instrument.

It is our guitar body, the carefully selected wood of our soul, the music of our genius, the hum of our love.

Listening with resonance is an art; the riff of a late night sax on the streets of New York City. It acknowledges discovery, invention, curiosity and retreat. It isn't interested inwhat makes sense. It cannot be quoted. It has a soap bubble in the air quality in that just when you think you have it, you've missed it. Resonant listening requires that you are fully present, willing to go where you've never

gone, willing to believe what all your theories have taught you to doubt. Resonant listening bonds you as if you no longer can tell who is talking, who listening.

It is the field of laughter, the reservoir of tears. You only know there is no beginning and there is no end, and no purpose and no rules. Resonant listening takes you down the rabbit hole of Wonderland, into Theseus's labyrinth and out of Plato's cave. It is a land of mystery where connecting is not of this world.

A child waking from a bad dream doesn't need you to get the facts right. She needs you to tilt your head in the manner of an Indian who, when listening for a train coming, listened to the vibrations in the ground, miles off, resonating with the energy. Resonance in relationships is mostly missed. Some of us hear words and lock onto them. Caught by reason, logic and the structure of our language – practical, cash-based, timed – we can't hear the murmur of the stars, even now as we speak.

A nice image of the difference is caught in the book of Job in the Old Testament.

Job after many losses and hugely struggling with his faith has listened to the theories of his friends. The theories make sense. The theories are beside the point. In the end Job, facing the deep resonance of his relationship with God says, "I have heard of thee with the hearing of my ear, but now my eye seeth thee." perhaps could be translated this way, "but now I get thy resonance."

See, hear, feel, taste, touch, imagine, tremble and wonder… all avenues to resonance, the music of loving. For loving is not only a language made of words, a hormone rush or a declaration of intention. It is surrender and surrender again to the soul music of our birth, the universal resonance of creation itself.

We like to teach couples a metaphor that captures the difference between understanding and resonance. We say it is possible to live your relationship as if in a garden where sun and rain and good earth support the growth of beautiful flowers and nourishing vegetables. We don't argue with gardens, we work them, care for them and enjoy them.

If not a garden, your relationship can become a courtroom where logic dominates, evidence is gathered, attorneys for the prosecution argue with attorneys for the defense. There will be guilty pleas and sentences granted. A judge will determine outcomes. It will strive to be fair. No resonance allowed.

In the early morning as you walk in your garden the smallest drop of dew on the petal of a rose will draw your attention. The buzzing of insects will awaken a hunger in you and the light and warmth of the sun reassure you of the fecundity of the earth. Your reverence will harmonize with your intention and gratitude will be your food.

The three-year-old boy came out of his room buck naked and stood in the huge family room as his father sweated and worked to install a stereo system. Ready for testing he was playing a Bob Dylan album and he had it cranked. Standing on a ladder fussing with some wires he could barely hear his son talking. He climbed down, turned the music down just a little and shouted, "I can't hear you."

His son, standing in the majesty of a three-year-old's authority said, "I can't have that music."

His father said, "It's Dylan. I love this music. Shut your door if you don't want to listen." His son still majestic, unafraid said, "I can't have that music." It went like that, back and forth several times, the father growing increasingly amazed at the authority and clarity of his son.

Finally, he said, "Okay, I'll turn it off" and he replaced Dylan with a classical album. In a few minutes his son again came out of his room, looked at his father and said, "I can have that music."

The vibes are always there, calling us to connect, to hear, to resonate with each other. If you can give in to full attentiveness, intimate conversation awaits you. If you cannot, every day will look a lot like yesterday.

If listening is critical and you can learn to get a sense of what journey you're on, if you can ground and re-ground your love and work intelligently with seven foundational principles as a philosophy that honors the legitimacy of each of your needs, you've begun to create the building blocks of long term and continually growing intimacy (I like to call this "sustainable enthusiasm" — the song lovers sing).

You'll need to know something of the genius you bring to this love and you'll need to tune in to the pathway to legitimacy, your own self-worth. All of this calls for leadership. The willingness to lead is fundamental to working with conflict and change.

G. Leadership

I know of no one who talks about leadership within marriage. It is a concept we usually connect with business, sports, the military or politics. But why confine this idea related to influence, energy and responsibility to those domains? I think it was John Maxwell who said "A leader is someone who creates the reality (that) others live in." This definition captures one of the *five intentions* that we all bring to relationship.

Didn't we start out thinking that we were capable of contributing seriously to our partner's happiness as they would to ours? Didn't we imagine that our love, gifts, sensitivities, vision and hard work would create a world that would surround our partners with joyful and meaningful days?

1. The Five Intentions

I believe we all bring some form of the five intentions to the alter of our marriage. Here they are:

1. We intend to co-create a richer and more meaningful reality for each of us to live within.

2. We intend to love each other unselfishly.

3. We intend to build a kingdom on earth that manifests our joint vision.

4. We intend to be there for each other in times of need, sickness, challenges or radical change.

5. We intend to evolve through life's natural developmental stages keeping our hands on the "Ariadne's thread" of our love.*

Leadership can be seen in all five. Each intention (and others you add) captures a need for action, for shaping the days we share and for responding to what's coming our way.

There's a distinction you might want to play with when talking about leadership in marriage. You may have been sidetracked in considering this idea because of old school ideas of leadership.

When we talk of leadership some people think of a high handed principle or an army drill sergeant. It was a "my way or the highway" kind of leadership, top down, right or wrong, your opinion doesn't matter, only your compliance (obedience) does.

That kind of leadership, non democratic, non consensual, no "buy in" required, was effective in driving people to extraordinary accomplishments – marines charging a hill under heavy fire, workers building massive projects in spite of the dangers.

It may still have its place under certain extreme conditions, but business leaders, educators, even high level coaches in college and professional sports are discovering a new world in which leadership looks more like an invitation than an order.

Ariadne was the mythical lover and saviour of Theseus of Athens. The thread from her ball of flax was the instrument of escape from the labyrinth for both of them. (To enjoy this story read *The King Must Die* by Mary Renault)

The idea of democracy isn't limited to political systems but has vast implications for marriage and family life. To go beyond entrenched models of power, the aristocracy in Europe for example, great social upheavals were necessary. It was necessary to change the conditions of power so that individuals might organize and rise in power through the rule of law and social and political change.

Likewise, sexism, racism and ageism have to be exposed and abolished in order for a truly representative political system and business culture to thrive. We are still a work in progress.

Within the family the idea that parents could abuse their children in the name of God's will or that fathers could unilaterally rule on economic affairs weakened as more and more individuals took democratic ideas and ideals seriously. We're not through yet.

A new model of leadership was emerging. The 60s and early 70s opened the door for a new conversation around change. This new model slowly began to take individual contributions seriously. It incorporated social science research and tuned into vast global economic changes as well. But what's most noteworthy is the freeing up of individual creativity and initiative – leadership from the bottom up.

It looks like this. Small integrated and focused teams outperform the older top down style of team management. Increasingly, individual genius is honored, invited, cultivated and empowered. Teams experience higher performance levels.

Vision works when the invitation to "buy in" is credible. The "buy in" involves the embrace of conflict which itself forces the evolution of vision. Effective "buy in" means that diversity of opinion is welcomed, objections are honored and communication is elevated so that the true essence of the vision is manifest.

Companies that thrive implement a leadership style that is fluid, mobile, present or real time. These companies have instant access to critical data (they are competent in business intelligence) and move towards manifesting their business "pitch" (they are competent in telling their story) in terms the world finds, not only attractive, buy meaningful.

Leaders learn that positional leadership is ineffective, that giving orders slows down productivity rather than speeds it up, and that teams need to develop their own esprit and their own vision all the while aligned with the larger vision of a company.

Leadership coaches who notice that a more precise way to define leadership effectiveness is whether a leader is "in" or "out" of leadership, not whether or not he was called a leader, also begin teaching new leadership competencies.

We begin to see that psychological factors of individual leaders shape their commitment to a set of beliefs about leadership. In order to unmask those factors, coaches themselves have to evaluate their own lives – their motives, intentions, natural genius, doofusness, triggers and, dare I say it, quality of their loving. They have to learn new competencies that invite (rather than lecture) leaders into a collaborative style and help them define a new way of imagining leadership.

Being "in" leadership means that a leader is present, not triggered by mood, not reactive, is available to the situation at hand, confident, open to input, attuned to the individual gifts (natural genius) of his team, honoring of his or her team and in gratitude for their efforts.

"Out" of leadership means a leader is easily triggered into unilateralism, moodiness or retaliation. An out of leadership leader is authoritarian, perhaps sexist, racist or some other predisposed lack of relatedness and human empathy.

These two distinctions indicate an inner grounding (leader is connected to their own legitimacy) or lack of it (leader is adrift, ungrounded, a spiritual orphan). Further, out of leadership leaders are stuck in a psychology of false images – "people are lazy," "they just don't care anymore," "they're all nine to fivers."

"In leadership" leaders are grounded in their own legitimacy and, therefore, can recognize and relate to the legitimacy of the individuals in their teams – "We'll put Mary in a situation where she can succeed," "Bob's challenge is he doesn't communicate well, we'll help him with that."

While it is true that grounded leaders go "in" and "out" of leadership (they are human) ungrounded leaders (orphans) do the same. No one is totally grounded and few are total orphans. The work is to notice the conditions under which you are tempted out of leadership and the conditions under which you are triggered into leadership.

2. Marriage Is a Laboratory

Marriage is, if you will, a leadership lab among other things. Two individuals each with their own natural genius, skill sets and talents come together with high standards for the life they want to create together. They may not realize it when their hormones are flowing, but their individuality and uniqueness will sooner or later force them to take look at the challenges of their lives through the perspective of their own emerging individual needs as well as leadership competencies.

One may see the need for an intense focus on their handling of money. If they don't want to go the old authoritarian way and create an ongoing power struggle about who's right and who is wrong they will have to create a conversation between equals concerning the challenge of dealing with money.

One will have more skill at initiating a conversation; one may have a better instinct (genius) for leading it. Leadership will look like an intentional invitation to brainstorm in perhaps a fairly structured way so that both partners are honored, heard and, in their own way, lead

Not an easy thing to do. We teach couples every single day how to get this conversation going. Leadership within marriage shows up in many ways. Couples who have given up on their marriage are often begging for one or the other to lead. The one who can be "in" leadership might suggest coaching or might reframe issues in a way that opens a path to continue.

Notice this: In matters sexual, leadership always looks invitational, never demanding. The frustrated partner may want to analyze or diagnose, demand or complain, become manipulative or pout but the road to reunion is a carefully explored road of curiosity, exploration and invitation. More on this later.

Leadership can look like an invitation to return to the love that got you started in the first place or it can focus on creating a brand new invitation to embrace the goodness of the relationship while agreeing to address the considerable challenges you are facing.

Here's an example. Everyone knows that men and women compete. I've noticed that competition in my own marriage wears several faces. Sometimes we compete over which movie is the better choice, other times we compete over the best route to a friend's house.

We compete over what one of our children really needs, or over who works harder around the house. It can be fun to compete or it can lead to bitterness. I've even heard couples compete over who loves the other more. What's important is what happens in the competition – does someone win and someone lose? Is there shaming, blaming or name calling? Competition is often just a desperate call for leadership.

On a rare day when the gods shined their light on me I led. My wife and I were invited to an elegant wedding at an upscale country club which it seemed to me was well hidden in the Santa Monica mountains. I'm a kid from the city and not particularly self-assured in situations where I think everyone else has a better idea of what's expected than I do; a classy wedding at a prestigious country club rattles me. My anxiety level goes up and when that happens my inner compass quits. I am, under the best circumstances, directionally challenged – I must have clear directions to even have a chance of finding my destination – but under circumstances of increased anxiety, my compass shuts down altogether.

We, that is, I, was lost. Didn't know north or south, east or west, and as darkness fell became frightened that we would never make it to the wedding. My fear in this instance shows up as low-level anger. My partner, Connecticut raised, elegantly dressed, though not anxious at all about upscale parties, made gentle suggestions as to the road we perhaps ought to consider taking. I could not listen. Finally, I stopped the car. We were at an impasse. I had no idea where we were or how to proceed. She sat quietly.

There are some moments in life when you're grateful for a voice, not your own, but one that leads you out of the mess you're in. From somewhere within came these words "You know, why don't you drive. You have a better sense of direction than I do. I'm turning this over to you."

Her response surprised me. "You don't have to be like that," she almost hissed. "Like what?" I protested. "Sarcastic," she said.

I explained that I was not being sarcastic. I realized just then what I should have admitted millennia ago – I am not the one to do directions. Competing with her originated in an old paradigm, an old leadership style. The act of surrender came easily that night and I've never wavered. What a joy it is to go somewhere today and simply ask my navigator to lead.

Surrender and genuineness are bedfellows here. The power of surrender must be understood. It is the power of true humility together with the resilience of transparency.

Simple capitulation, passive aggressively giving in, tolerating or patronizing will only further fuel the underlying lack of trust that started the competitiveness in the first place.

Accommodation and passive compliance are fear-based and will only serve to keep the mistrust going. Whether you're in a business environment or in a conversation with your partner, notice that leadership requires you to be 100% honest with yourself first. Once you're there, you can speak in a straightforward way with a clear mind.

Leadership within marriage honors each partner's natural genius, recognizes where each of you is a bozo, listens carefully to the message within the drama of emotion, pays attention to triggers and consistently manifests honor and gratitude for the partner of your choice.

Here are a few observations that tell me when I'm **"out" of leadership:**

- I'm out when I react instead of respond to an emotionally loaded event.

- I'm out when I whine, worry or live in the past.

- I'm out when I diagnose, analyze, hypothesize or theorize – or in any other way distance myself from her in the present moment.

- I'm out when I indulge fear of what might happen.

- I'm out when I sulk.

I'm **"in" leadership** when:

- I stop, look and listen to those around me.

- I proactively problem solve.

- I fully expect myself to love the one I've chosen to love regardless of her mood or situation.

- I indulge no exit strategies such as "I knew this wouldn't work" or "that's the way women are."

- I can naturally and non-competitively follow her natural genius leadership.

- My "embrace of conflict" leads to intimate connecting.

- I can connect to the bigger vision of our marriage and the long-term commitment I have for its success.

- I stay connected to Ariadne's connective thread of our love.

We'll create a guidebook to help you work your own way into this conversation.

Leadership in marriage simply calls for you to lead when you know what you're doing and you know who and where you are. And, it calls you to surrender or follow when your partner is leading. Kind of like dancing.

VIII. Transforming Marriage

We've considered several competencies that are necessary as skills or tools for fully claiming your marriage.

The competencies of self-esteem, understanding natural genius, the four disciplines that are critical to self grounding, listening competencies and the nature and importance of leadership – all provide a foundation for living in your marriage fully. We shift now to a focus on energy – the kind of energy you bring to relationships. Transforming ordinary energy into living fully in the present – in the *presence* of your marriage, a daily re-grounding of your intention, an energy that resonates with the very resonance of creation - creates the substance of intimate connecting.

We'll look at the energy aspects of marginality, comment on faithfulness and revisit commitment as it shows up in your philosophy of marriage and vows. And there's a strategy we'll present, in moving from assumptions to intimate connections that we call CAPPS. All this is meant to move you toward the competency of becoming increasingly competent in transforming your marriage.

The first rule among all other principles for transforming marriage from marginal to magnificent, from drone to song, from ordinary to extraordinary – is this: *You may not, either of you, have an exit strategy.*

The number of individuals who fool themselves into believing that "They'll work on this a little longer and if he/she doesn't change, I'll…" is significant. They've bought into an illusion.

That illusion is that any change whatsoever can happen when one person has one foot out of the relationship.

For this reason, the first thing I do is ask a couple who wants magnificence if they will commit a minimum of time – perhaps a year – and during that time will absolutely not consider separation or divorce.

Exit strategies are walking illusions. They keep you from embracing the full power of your own individuality and *your* own love. They keep you from challenging your partner in a way that honors *their* love and exit strategies are a self-imposed lie – an inner lie – that undermines your integrity.

Leadership can transform marriage. Conflict can be the vehicle of huge change. Loving is perhaps the greatest fuel on earth for transformation, and perhaps the least appreciated or understood, but all rely on this simple truth that risk, being fully present and committed to being fully present, is indispensible for change.

Marriages can move from dysfunctional to functional, from mediocre to making it, or prefer to say, from marginal to magnificent. We aim for marriages that sing because your love deserves it, the world needs it, and children everywhere will thrive because of it – they will be safer, healthier and more likely to reach their full potential if you embrace the full possibilities in your marriage and encourage others to do the same Exit strategies are clever devices that deprive you of realizing the possibility of a healthy marriage. So don't worry where you are on a scale of marginal to magnificent, wherever you are you can realize more. It's a promise built in from birth. But just to remind you of a few road signs pointing to a need for change rather than a need to end, here again, are some indicators of marginality:

Marginal Marriages

- If you do not share a clear, articulated vision for your marriage – it is marginal.

- If you aren't competent in conflict and cannot embrace it, and instead are prone to chronic and repetitive arguments – it is marginal.

- If the light has dimmed, the energy is low and interesting conversation infrequent – it is marginal.

- If you can't tell me, in three minutes time, what your partner cherishes, admires or values about you – it is marginal.

- If intimate conversations – spiritual, emotional, psychological or physical – happen less and less often, your marriage is marginal.

- If your vows and commitments are not an integral part of your intimate conversations – your marriage is marginal.

Let's expand a little on these observations:

- Vision to live in the micro-community of marriage and to extend your intentions outward into your community.

- Embracing conflict is a fundamental skill (and talent) for those who want their marriages to sing.

- Marriages, like the people in them, can become depressive.

- Do you celebrate each other?

- The creation of (sacred) space and time for reconnecting is critical to your marriage.

- Promises are self-talk that show up in vows and undermines your belief in yourselves and your choice of partner.

Without vision, celebration, sacred space and time for reconnecting, without the competency to embrace conflict and rethink your philosophy of marriage – couples can easily be seduced by "maybe we should end this." But it's not ending that most of us need, it is beginning.

Faithfulness

Our society makes much of the need for faithfulness. Many marriages fail because one partner wanders. What is faithfulness? How does it relate to the fully consciously living of your vows?

Betrayal is common. All of us have been left out, left down, tricked, deceived or manipulated so that we felt a huge sense of loss. We know the pain when someone we love is not who we thought they were but someone else entirely. Longing for a relationship we can count on, for someone we can trust completely who will not trick us, lie to us, abandon or fool us – is clearly part of the human condition. This longing, however, may be at the heart of much unfaithfulness.

Here's a story. When Judy and Bob married she felt incredibly fortunate. She said, "I've found my life's soul mate." He was her ideal. Bob was a man of high standing in the community, a professional, warm and articulate. She knew he was quality, a relational boy scout. She celebrated the relationship with every friend who would listen.

Their wedding was a huge and joyous party. Friends, family and neighbors all gathered at the beach for what truly seemed like a perfect match. Soon Judy was coaching other women on how to find the perfect mate. She considered writing a book about their meeting, did a couple of local talk show interviews and began to record her thoughts on their marriage on tape.

Their marriage was "made in heaven" she said and she would do everything in her power to please Bob and to show him how grateful she was to have him.

Bob did the same. He regaled friends with stories of the perfect match. "We're so compatible," he'd say. "She seems to know what I'm going to say before I say it. The sex is unbelievable. I've never had a relationship like this." He'd offer advice to his friends on duplicating his experience. He'd comment on their choice of women, steer them towards choices that would likely end up with supreme happiness like his own.

I met Judy and Bob just after they discovered the affair. They were married just under six years. When they told me how they started out I asked "What happened?"

Bob said he was smothered by her idealization of him. "I'm nice but not that nice," he told me. He said that the more he tried to become the individual that he really is the more Judy tried to shape him into the man she thought he was and could be. Judy's take was that Bob was a narcissistic little boy. She said she tried to encourage him to live his life fully but he misunderstood her and soon saw all she did and said as an attempt to control him. Neither of them were aware of how narcissistic their original attraction really was. It's easy to see in another person the qualities you would like to see and it's common to blame them when they don't become what you expect of them.

It would have helped them be sober about their loving if they had taken some time to explore what they were seeing, or thought they were seeing, in each other.

A. Vows and a Consciously Created Philosophy of Marriage

We think vows are a vital part of the process of partnering because they potentially contain a window into your philosophy of marriage. They hold out the best of who you are and who you want to become. They also create the opportunity for revealing who you aren't. Vows anchor intention and hold you in partnership while you grow and as the world around and within you inevitably changes.

It's common for couples to forget what they vowed at the ceremony. It's uncommon to see or hear couples relating to their vows as if those vows were a critical statement about who they are individually and what their marriage is about.

This may be because their vows were never theirs in the first place or they never integrated their intentions into their daily married life once the wedding party was over. We all may want to do an upgrade regarding our vows. We'll need to think it through. Here are some questions for you to ask as you consider your own vows.

- Who am I talking to?

- Who do I want to be for him/her?

- What does my marriage expect of me?

- Who else is listening?

- How do my vows relate to my deepest held values?

- How do I want to deal with change?

- Do I need my partner to agree with the beliefs and values contained in my vows?

- If we have children, how will these vows support their right to be loved and their right to be individuals?

- Who are the relevant communities who would share an interest in our vows?

Here are a few comments meant not so much to explain the above questions but to expand them.

- When creating my vows am I primarily talking to myself about my own values or am I considering who my partner is – their vulnerabilities, needs, gifts and fears.

- How do I want to show up in this marriage? What ideals do I live within? What do I say about my needs, vulnerabilities, gifts and fears?

- Consider your marriage as a third person with a voice of its own. What does your marriage need and what does it expect?

- Am I talking to a former partner that perhaps I mistreated?

- What drives my desire to partner? What do I stand up for regardless of anyone's approval or disapproval?

- Do my vows allow for growth and expansion while supporting continuity and stability in this relationship?

- Can I stand up for my vows regardless of my partner's changes?

- Will my children be blessed by my living my vows?

- Name the communities that this marriage will participate in. How do I want to invite their participation in this marriage's well being?

Use these questions as springboards to writing your own questions. Dialogue with each other out loud. Brainstorm. Create conversations around commitments that aren't legalistic or punitive. Ask a lot of questions of each other. Let time pass and ask some more. Dream about it. Talk to others you trust. Allow your deepest wisdom to manifest in the creation of your vows.

Vows can and should be a working philosophy that is woven throughout the life of your marriage. They should evolve as they more accurately reflect who you are as you deepen and grow. Vows are the "coin of the realm" and form one foundation (the philosophy of the marriage) for your life together. Vows remind me of a conversation with a close friend about flying an airplane.

He was a pilot in WWII, flying a P51. He told me he would often take his plane up when they weren't flying missions and put the hood on so that he couldn't see anything but his instruments. In this way he learned to trust his instruments in times of confusion, bad weather or extreme trauma. Many pilots weren't able to do this and crashed.

Vows are sort of like flying blind in that you trust what you've committed to in times of uncertainty, bad weather or calamity. They guide you through the dark times and energize you in the light.

Marginal marriages happen for a lot of reasons. One of the most important, in our observations, is an almost total lack of understanding of what marriage *is* and what it's *for*.

The need to publicly proclaim our intentions is part of the substance of love. It invites the community to partner with us in supporting our (new) micro-community. It proclaims our deepest intention to live by our word and to cherish each other. It opens the door to our own contribution to our own community.

Here's a sample of generic vows taken off the Internet:

"I take you to be my friend, my lover, the mother of my children, my wife. I will be yours in times of plenty and in times of want, in times of sickness and in times of health, in times of joy and in times of sorrow, in times of failure and in times of triumph. I promise to cherish and respect you, to care for and protect you, to comfort and encourage you, and stay with you, for all eternity."

Good words. Nothing wrong with them. But if we played around a little with this form of vows we could take them to another level of response – response ability.

"I will be a friend to you, your lover who loves you even when you do not feel lovable or feel your love for me. If we are blessed with children I will participate fully in fathering them and support you in every way as you mother them (or, I will mother them to the best of my ability always conscious of you as their father). There will be times of plenty and times of want, there will be sickness as well as health – I will work alongside you and not live in fear of failure but instead use it as an opportunity for learning and growth. I will not rest in success and use it to separate myself from others we love, but test every success against the long-range vision we share. I cherish you now and will throughout our marriage. I promise to treat you with the respect you deserve, to care for you and protect you to the fullest of my energies. I will comfort, challenge and encourage you throughout our time here and beyond this life."

Vows are meant to be your creation, born out of your love, reflective of your individual and joint intention and capable of expressing your deepest purpose. Marriage is about the resonance of love. It is also a carrier of vision that extends to the community and to the meaning and legacies of your lives. Healthy marriages create healthy communities. They are micro world changers.

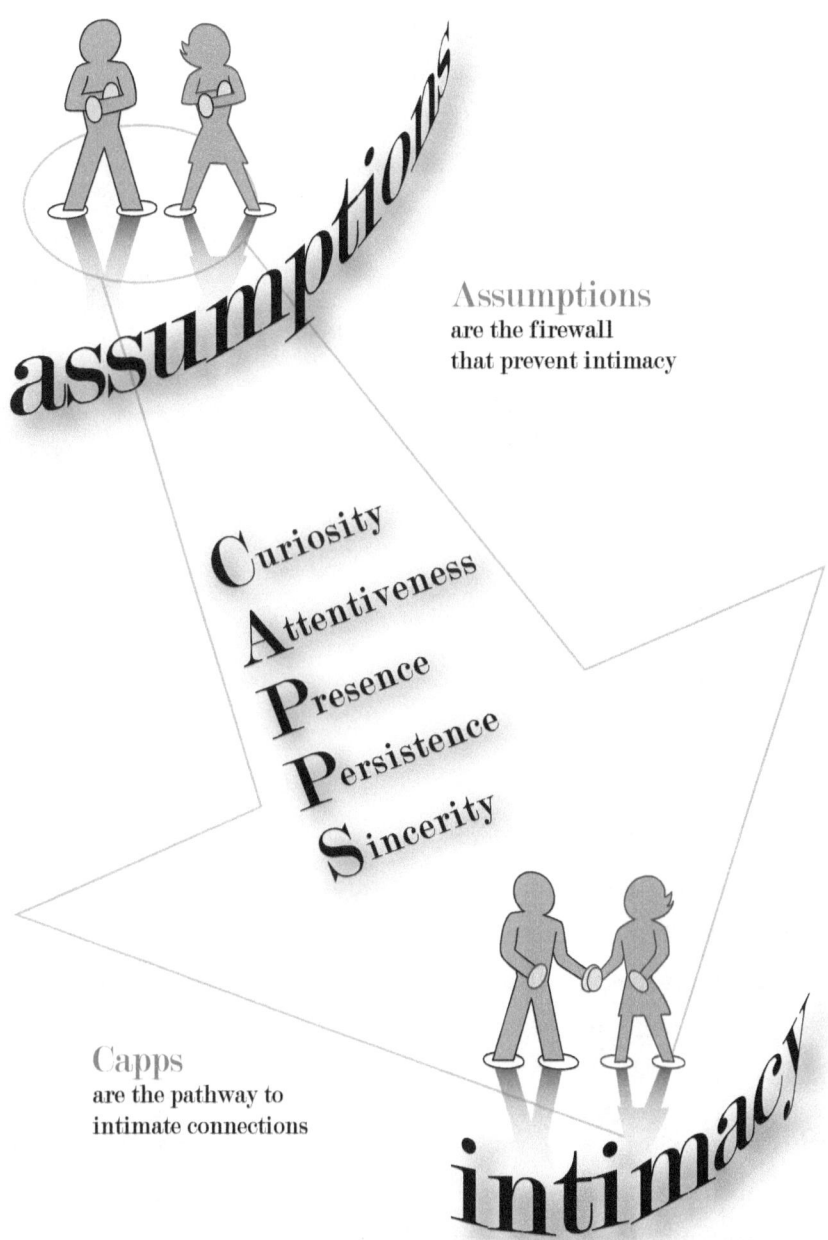

Assumptions
are the firewall
that prevent intimacy

Curiosity
Attentiveness
Presence
Persistence
Sincerity

Capps
are the pathway to
intimate connections

B. The CAPPS Model

Creating the necessary conditions for moving from "assumptive isolation" to "collaborative intimacy."

To fully capitalize on the power of consciously created vows and to embody (incorporate) them in the fabric of your daily life requires a few skill sets and a talent for doing the work.

We created the CAPPS model as a reminder of some basics we would need to keep us tracking. CAPPS looks like this:

C: Curiosity.

A: Attentiveness.

P: Presence.

P: Persistence.

S: Sincerity. On the left side of a sheet of paper vertically write: Assumptions. On the right, vertically write: Intimacy. Between these two you can write the five vehicles for moving across the page, from assumptions to intimacy. What it takes to do that is this.

Curiosity. Curiosity kills the cat, the old saying warns, but it's not entirely accurate. In fact, it may be the essence of a cat's life. Curiosity about your partner is an antidote to blame, shame, diagnosis, criticism and judgment.

A line from a Stafford poem comes to mind: "who are you really, stranger?" Curiosity about your partner need not be invasive – a private eye type of thing. Curiosity is having genuine interest in the person sitting across the table from you.

Many mistakes have been made that confuse nosing around with curiosity. Some people can't or don't trust their partner. They have a lot of work to do in disentangling their fear of trusting from their early childhood learning, their wounds or their history in this relationship. All of it needs to be addressed before you can enjoy the benefits of genuine curiosity.

Curiosity looks like serious interest in your partner's point of view, their nuanced attitudes, their deep passion and their curiosity. Without curiosity conversations become linear and predictable, sexual intimacy becomes routine and spiritual sharing flat lines. Curiosity opens, deepens and penetrates. Each of us feel touched when in the presence of someone who is genuinely curious about who we are. Of course, it takes discipline to be curious and to stay with it. I know a man who described his great fortune in being married to the woman who is his wife by saying this, "She teaches me there is no blame, no shame, no judgment. Only discovery. Whenever I fail, she simply wants to know what happened and asks, 'You okay?'"

He went on, "She teaches me every day and I can say with certainty that I've changed my life and my effectiveness as a business leader because of her."

Curiosity is also an effective tonic for power struggles. Instead of trying to win, ask. Ask your partner questions about their point of view and why their point of view is so very important to them.

Along with curiosity is **attentiveness.** You may think that they are pretty much the same but they are not. Attentive curiosity means you

183

have the discipline to stay with your intention. I have often observed couples who begin with what looks like genuine curiosity only to change it quickly into diagnosis. They gather a little information, yet can't sustain their intention. They grab onto a word or idea and quickly begin analyzing their partner.

They may think they are being curious but their curiosity only serves their pre-existing theories about their partner. Attentiveness means you suspend your theories, diagnoses, analyses and listen with that "third ear" to what is being revealed.

"I'm curious but I have to admit I know what he's going to say before he says it. I've always been able to read him better than he can read himself." This woman, married twenty-two years, complained that her husband was a "poor communicator."

She had excellent language skills (she was a practicing family therapist) but not a lot of humility or patience. Our work circled around helping him create some space for himself where he could believe that what he had to say and the way he had of saying it was legitimate in its own right. He needed to attend to his own presence before he could begin to successfully attend to what she was saying. She, on the other hand, needed to begin recognizing that her assumptions were undermining their communication as well.

Attentive curiosity will not sing without **presence.** He had learned a long time ago that, when it came to women, his presence was secondary to what they had to say.

Presence is born of believing in your own legitimacy. If you indulge a kind of orphan psychology and believe that you have little right to be heard, seen or noticed, than your presence will be a weak signal and other stations will not be able to pick you up.

"Move over world and give me some sky, I've got me some wings I'm eager to try ... you're gonna hear from me." (Inside Daisy Clover).

It was Emile Zola who said, "You ask me what I came into this world to do and I will tell you. I came to live out loud."

Presence and your deep belief in your right to embrace your own legitimacy are the necessary conditions for genuine attentive curiosity.

Persistence is the juice that carries the tune. Some give up easily. "While I am interested in what she has to say, it seems most of the time I've heard it all before." We would say that he simply doesn't listen. If he does listen, he doesn't listen carefully. If he listens carefully, he probably isn't curious about pieces of the conversation he doesn't understand. If he is curious, he probably makes decisions about relevance long before she's through.

He may want to be seen as listening but is quite possibly lazy. He may think he's interested but instead is listening to the theater in his own head. In any case, he isn't persistent in focusing on the stranger standing before him.

Persistence means you have to question your own intention. You have to go beyond the surface chatter you've reassured yourself with since the beginning of the marriage. If you want "songs in the night" you'll have to learn to dance. Persistence means you'll commit to a deeper listening intention than you've practiced before.

And all of these – curiosity, attentiveness, presence and persistence – must be grounded in a fundamental dimension of your character. That basis is called **sincerity**; it is the quality of genuineness. Genuineness is overwhelmingly evident in a child. Healthy children are who they are. They capture us because there is no guile, no charade, no posturing. If a child is curious about you, she'll be transparently so. If he's attentive, whether to a beetle, a dust ball or your face, he will be fully so. Children are fully present in the moment, persistent in their interest and genuine in their love. When you meet a child who lacks one or more of these, you can be pretty sure an adult has had something to do with it.

CAPPS can move you from assumptions to intimate relating. Not the mere insight but the disciplined practice of it. Pay attention to what you bring to each conversation and you'll soon notice another potentially transforming reality – the presence of fear.

C. The Disarming of Fear

Fear is underappreciated as a relationship stopper. Fear can be as subtle as the morning fog or as threatening as an Atlantic storm. Fear stops relationships when it is not noticed, named or faced. Criticism of your partner is often based in fear but instead of noticing the fear you intellectualize it – i.e., you serve the ego – and out comes the knife blades of analysis. You may be reasonable you may even be right (after all, all of us can be quite easily diagnosed) but your false ego will simply have grown. Your relationship will suffer; the natural consequence of criticism/diagnosis will be defensiveness. This, of course, leads to contempt as the egos join in battle which eventually will cause you to entirely abandon the love, which connected you in the first place. By the time you walk into my office both of you will be certain that "everything would be good if only you were willing to change."

Fear in relationship is learned. A team of researchers once noticed that infants are only frightened by two things, a loud noise or sudden loss of support. We didn't start out being fearful but we soon learned to be. Many parents believe fear is the only way to shape their child's behavior. Some years ago, a middle-aged man asked me to tell him how hard to spank his child. He hit his three-year-old with his hand but a pastor had told him to use only a stick or belt, "that way he won't take it personally," the pastor said, but instead would connect the punishment with the bad behavior.

There are all sorts of crazy advice drifting around out there and most of it is based on the fear of losing control. The insecure ego, the shallow lover, the need to project motives on others, all obscure the real thing that is happening. In adult relationships, we bring our history of fear and our conditioning so that habit converts a simple feeling into a fear-based strategy.

Perhaps the pastor had, himself, been raised in an environment of fear. Perhaps the adults were out of control or were raised by parents who were out of control. Perhaps no one emphasized the power of loving, understanding, empathy, good authoritative coaching or the capacity to see the child. When fear teaches fear, fear-based behavior results. From this we see resentment, anger, dishonesty and more.

To disarm fear you'll have to first become aware of its presence. It's not about doing something about it as much as it is unmasking it. Let yourself feel your fear when you

find yourself in an emotionally challenging situation. Feel it, and then proceed with what you have to say. Just the facts, no embellishment. Like this. "Last night when you came home later than expected I was aware that I missed you. Additionally, I was fearful that something bad might have happened."

You won't have to create a lecture or sermon about responsibility. You won't have to educate your partner on etiquette either. All you have to do is be. No drama. No punishment. No threats. In doing this, you'll open a space for transformation.

It's plain to see that disarming fear will require certain communication competencies. In this next section, I'm going to remind you of the power of the journeys model to facilitate communication.

D. Communication

The *With These Rings* model offers a new paradigm of marriage for couples to work within. Remember, it has three foundations. These include the three journeys in marriage; the needs-based philosophy of marriage; and the garden of your love. Each contain a unique energy.

The three journeys are based in the three domains of relating. They are: *outer world* or roommates – the domain of here and now that includes practical living considerations such as dealing with money, space and time; *inner world* – the domain that addresses the "Who am I?" question and includes the importance of your history, your symbolic life, your emotional I.Q., spiritual life, natural genius and more; and, finally, the domain of intimate relating, the *shared world* – the sacred space and sacred time you jointly create to explore, discover and expand your deepest connectedness.

We intentionally use the word journeys for journeys not only require energy but create it as well. It looks to us that upon marrying, couples simultaneously enter several kinds of adventures. There is the establishment of your kingdom here on earth. You begin to focus on what kind of home you want to create, what things you'll need to make it happen, to make it harmonize with an inner vision you each brought to the altar of your marriage. This first domain holds our focus to living successfully in this world. Not to overwork the point, but notice the energy-based words: adventure, focus, create, make it happen, harmonize, successfully.

In the first journey, you'll begin to look at division of labor, the use of space, how to create wealth and other earthbound issues matters.

The language of this first domain has a kind of "hard hat and lunch pail" quality. The more direct and efficient the language, the better. It is also a language you bring from your own experience in your family of origin and couples frequently become awake to a need to examine their assumptions and ideas in this domain.

Arguments in this domain often originate in the identification with attitudes and styles learned before the couple met each other. These attitudes tend to calcify energy and deprive the relationship of energy needed for the challenges of this domain.

There is a sense of one's way of approaching life being threatened. Simply facing the attitudes learned earlier in life and admitting them to each other opens the door to new dialogue that doesn't have a power struggle dimension to it.

My family was poor and we often worried about our simplest needs being met. My partner's family, while not affluent, was affluent by my standards. She doesn't remember ever having to worry about there being ample resources for clothes or food. Vacations were a novel idea in my family.

She approaches life with a positive attitude about money and doesn't focus on lack or its possibility. I worry a lot. We've had to develop (i.e., create) ways of talking about our finances that honor both of our histories and that would move us into dealing with money in the present tense.

Naturally, this takes us into the second domain. To fully appreciate the depth of my fear, I've had to discard my tendency to project insensitivity onto her and instead work to articulate the nature of my fear (energy attached to a negative experience or image), as well as "grow up" in my ability to live in this present world. I am learning that her attitudes have real value in our family. She helps me be generous. She takes me toward embracing our larger family celebrations with abundance instead of fear.

The communication challenge here is to separate my past learning from our current situation. Her challenge might be something like listening to the wisdom of my financial conservatism. Communication works when projections are withdrawn, when active listening is happening, when we discipline ourselves to a weekly business meeting and when we establish continuity with our discussion of shared vision.

Communication (commune/community/common) means you both recognize that you are a lot alike. Both have fears, both want goodness, neither of you are truly lazy or indifferent, and both of you want your love to be present, full of energy and working. You go toward an entirely new level of communication when you consider entering the third domain. We'll get to that but first I want to say something about how domain awareness leads to thinking about these things like a journey.

In the first domain, you are problem solving, planning and acting in a kind of one-dimensional world. That includes income, budget, basic needs and long-range hopes. This first domain begins to look like a journey (and therefore changes the way you are able to talk about it) when you realize that you are jointly *creating* a life together that will profoundly impact the quality of aging, the lives of your children, your relationships with your extended family, the possibility of legacies, your involvement with the various communities of choice and your impact on the well being of others.

Thinking of it as a journey captures a sense of adventure, challenge and vision. It reminds us that no plan, however well thought through, guarantees predictability. It helps us notice chance and reframe failure. It pulls us towards honoring each other's creative contributions and shapes this dimension of relationship as a shared work of art.

The idea of journey deepens our bond and helps us to look at the challenges of life through the same framework. It is part of "'til death do us part" and the quality of our shared journey is the lyricism of our song. Marriages that sing embrace the journeys within each domain. In the final section of this book we'll show you how each domain, as it becomes a journey, leads to a kind of "mini" marriage, the three of which make your marriage an ongoing concert.

The desire to relate intimately, to enjoy deep connection, is universal. Without it, every day looks a lot like yesterday. There is a language of loving (or perhaps there are languages of loving unique to each of us). We see the desire to connect as containing all the dimensions of intimacy – emotional, psychological, intellectual, spiritual and physical

– each with its own special take on language, its own energy and its own gifts. If any one dimension is neglected intimacy suffers.

But how do you get there when conversations in and around first domain considerations dominate so much of your time? Our time is easily used up by work, household maintenance and social obligations. If we are a family with children we may not see any way to create the space and time for our loving.

By Invitation Only, and Intentionally by Invitation

We descend into a shared intimate journey by inviting each other to do so. Initially, this was not difficult because our newness, attraction, chemistry and perhaps inner clock were driving a need to seriously connect with a partner. We fell in love. We may have lived for awhile in the illusion that the chemical cocktail we enjoyed was intimacy at its finest. Many believed they had truly broken through ordinary human barriers and were able to directly experience their lovers at oceanic depths of intimacy.

But time tells us otherwise. Life's demands will distract you, wounds happen, age happens.. How can we get back to the love we once knew, we ask. The answer is, that love in that form was historical fact and will not be duplicated. Its essence, however, was not an illusion and can be a point of reference as well as a source of deep nourishment for the maturing couple.

The journey into intimacy connects us with the reality of that love, as it exists in its present manifestation.

Here are the conditions for sustaining that journey successfully. **First,** each partner will have to be capable and willing to do his or her own *inner work.* This means they will embrace their own inner journey and commit to a lifetime of discovery. They will each take 100% responsibility for not only the discovery process but also for encountering what they discover and using it to deepen and develop their own sense of identity.

Second, each partner will pay attention to his or her own *unique language* for conveying this unfolding self-awareness. We each have natural genius in communicating aspects of our inner selves. It takes a willingness to focus on our own unique style of communication as well as courage to claim the individual legitimacy of our journey. This is the basic material of intimate sharing. It is why we called it sacred, since it comes from that deep inner spiritual space of unique personal origins – the soul of being.

Disclosure is a linguistic, interpersonal and leadership challenge. It means you are willing to put your very integrity and the integrity of your journey on the line. It means you chose to be vulnerable with your partner and in doing so offer to recognize her deepest vulnerabilities as well.

All of this involves an *awareness of transition*. If I am living intensely in the world of the first domain, focused on schedules, bills, soccer games and the weekly car wash, it will not naturally occur to me that there is a deeper need in this relationship, the ignorance of which will drive a kind of "drying up" of the potential joys of being roommates.

I may be seduced into diagnosing my partner. My ego may lure me towards critical analysis of her shortcomings. If, however, I am able to daily recognize that the promised Garden of Eden of our loving is in need of attention I am creating a huge first step in singing our marriage back into the promised land of connectedness.

I will need the competency of transitioning from one domain into another. You might say that a successful marriage is one of continuous transition from roommates to inner work, from intimacy to roommates, from inner work to intimacy, and so on. Transitioning is a competency; it's not astrophysics but you do need to notice it as a need.

E. Competency in Becoming Increasingly Competent

If a woman is stuck in adolescence she's likely to filter all her needs in such a way that they show up as wants. Her song will become a groan. Her partner will be unable to respond because her mode of operation will appear monotone. If a man is stuck in adolescence he's likely to be demanding, analytical, anxious and even hysterical. His song is muted. His partner will become defensive and depressive.

They cannot sing together because they have been unable to leave the house of their parents. They probably have surrounded themselves with other couples stuck in adolescence. They're good at video games, cynical humor and at avoiding relationships with mature couples. They don't trust anyone over 30.

We see this as a competency issue rather than terminal dysfunction. To begin to develop relational competency you must first admit that you are so incompetent that you don't realize you need relational competency. You really do believe that "being in love" is enough. You are "unconsciously incompetent."

A friend of mine, prominent in AA refused to talk to a man that I wanted to refer to AA. This man wanted to "cut down on his drinking" and I suggested he talk to my friend. When I called my friend to tell him someone would be calling him he started asking questions. He soon discovered that my referral was looking for a "tune up" not an overhaul.

He said this, "I don't really work with anyone who hasn't hit bottom. They may think they want help but usually are far from what it takes to change their lives. Your referral needs to take his elevator down a few more floors before he's ready for this work."

You might say that my referral was unconsciously incompetent and didn't know it yet. When he finally lost his job and his wife left him, was diagnosed with stomach ulcers as well as facing bankruptcy, he began to awaken to the reality of his incompetence. At that point, he didn't ask for my referral but found an AA meeting on his own.

Competence takes willingness and awareness. The couple, stuck in adolescence may have to endure many pointless arguments, cold nights and even separation before one of them begins to awaken. As Simon in *Lord of the Flies* reminds his friends, "Evil is not out there. It's in each of us."

In addition to willingness, competency requires a conscious decision to embrace change. The false ego will resist change, but if you can move into awareness of your own presence, including awareness of your feelings without indulging the desire to make your partner responsible for those feelings, then you have the possibility of changing the way you've thought about relationships. That is a small but important step towards becoming competent in increasing relational competency.

Notice, as you begin this work, the truth of a simple observation – *"you are what you focus on."*

Competency is an art and a skill set. Turning away from a diagnostic and critical attitude with your partner, or from self-criticism, or the "pleasure" of a depressed or angry mood – will open "space" for embracing awareness. Focusing on awareness will generate competency in self-encounter and relational disclosure. You will begin moving towards conscious incompetency and that allows for true intimate sharing.

Finally, competency is a leadership attribute. I once thought leadership was telling others how to behave. As I took my own elevator down several floors I discovered that leadership had most to do with the capacity to truly face myself and to treat others as if they were already doing the same. My superiority and indifference to the suffering of others became painfully obvious. My lack of empathy caused deep remorse.

I soon discovered that leadership in relationships looked like simply tending to my own work and having the courage to share myself with my partner. All this requires a strong connection to the roots of your loving. As we near the end of this book, there are a few stories that might help you connect with ideas and images that make your marriage sing.

IX. Tending the Roots

A. The Garden and The Courtroom

Walk outside and stop and look at the first flowers you see. They are there for you. They do not strain to be seen, do not call out about their relative beauty, "they do not toil nor do they spin," Jesus reminds us, yet, they are cared for and their beauty is exquisite. They have a legitimate right to be here.

Flowers remind us of the simplicity of being itself. They need sun, welcome rain, do well in harmony with other plants, give, with no demand for reciprocity. The garden was there long before we named it. The flowers came before human creations called attention to their beauty.

Relationships didn't begin with psychotherapists observing them. Humans have loved each other from the beginning of time. They mated, had children, experimented with different forms of relationship and under it all there was connectedness and the need for continuity.

The last century may have helped us understand some of the dynamics of relationships a little better but perhaps the profound advances in relationship competency we all long for are still a ways off. Perhaps we've grown more skilled intellectually in dissecting but with the skill, we have also grown more adept at living with distance. Our obsession with material goods, our needs for bigger and fancier homes and cars, our entertainment culture, our love of war – all do not indicate a growing relationship competency.

It sometimes seems to me that more couples live in a courtroom than in a garden. Their needs become a case before an invisible judge. They "hire" attorneys to prosecute and defend. They appeal to evidence of wrongdoing. They often sentence each other to weeks of coldness. They eat distance around the dining room table.

If the flowers need water they argue over "whose problem it is." The soil grows dry and parched, the weeds flourish and the trees no longer bear fruit. Is this because they no longer have anything in common? Is it because our society is transitory in nature and we've lost our ability to commit? I don't think so.

Storytelling and the use of metaphor has served humans well for thousands of years. Perhaps couples need not only a new paradigm – a new way to imagine marriage – but a reintroduction to the power of images held in stories and meant to point us not in the direction of lethal analysis of one another but in the direction of a broader and deeper understanding of our mutuality.

I "water" my marriage by taking a break from my necessary schedule and thinking for a moment or two about my partner – what might she be needing right now, when have I last connected, really connected with her on something other than roommate business, when have I noticed her?

Gardens help me remember that ordinary needs are not negotiable. When the roses need water they need water. When weeds are encroaching, the vegetables need me to remove them. When a fruit is ripe for the picking, it's ready and will not wait until tomorrow.

My love and my intention in marriage is to not only *tend* the garden of my marriage but to *be* the garden. I am resource and food to her, a place of delight and sometimes a chore. She is a garden to me. Together our energies, mutual commitment, varied interests, curiosity, deep needs, form an opportunity for mutual enrichment, shared vision and deep nourishment. "We come to each other," Wendell Berry reminds us.

Gardens contain a model for relationship because they remind us of all the things necessary for healthy interaction with our simplest and deepest needs. Our needs in relationship are not debatable even though they can't always be fully met. Our relationship is ever evolving, has its seasons, times for work and growth, time for harvest and even time for dormancy.

The power to enchant, I mentioned above, is that most of us are easily seduced by the promise of objectivity and all of us overestimate our own ability to be truly objective. So many arguments circle around one or both partners believing there's an objective truth here and if "he or she could only see it," we'd be fine.. The enchantment keeps the circular argument going. Lots of heat, little light.

These two powerful metaphors reflect an underlying model or paradigm of marriage. If you came into your marriage unwittingly believing in fairness, reason, the idea of victim and perpetrator, you probably live in an old and outdated paradigm of marriage. That paradigm has more in common with the courtroom than with a garden.

This is why adversarial divorce, obscenely expensive, still thrives in the United States. A more contemporary model, called collaborative divorce, more closely reflects that the human garden within marriage can, as well, be the need for compassionate ending when a marriage simply can no longer work.

Transforming your marriage from courtroom to garden is about more than "learning how to communicate" — much more, in fact. It's about exposing and challenging the paradigm you both use daily to try to succeed in an overly demanding world. Let me tell you a quick story.

A man and a woman went to see a therapist friend of mine because the husband had been caught ("red handed" she said) in an online highly seductive relationship. At first, he claimed innocence and later moved to "harmless flirting." She was outraged at his denial and felt deeply betrayed.

In their first session the therapist, mistakenly I think, allowed the husband to "go off" on his wife about her deficits as a woman. Mistaken, I think, not because he

shouldn't get to talk about what was wrong for him in their marriage but because first, he wasn't talking about himself, and second, a solid

Five Quick and Easy Steps to Improve Your Marriage

There's a ton of advice out there. Let's boil some of it down to basics. Here are five things you can do today to increase the quality of your loving:

1. Say your partner's name out loud three times. Then say three simple things out loud that you like about him or her.

2. Pick your favorite of these and email or phone message them with it immediately.

3. Create a surprise for your partner today. Ideas: pick up a book, pick a flower, do a chore that is normally theirs to do, listen three minutes without interrupting except to ask clarifying questions, draw a picture of you loving them, write a short poem.

4. Pull out an old picture of the two of you having fun, make a homemade frame (a friend did this with sticks from the yard) and place it by their dinner place.

5. Tell them of your dreams for this relationship.

Marriage is a work (of joy) in progress. Embrace your today.

ground of mutual trust had not been established between the couple or between the partners and the therapist.

At any rate, she was clearly in the courtroom of the mind and was really seeking confirmation from the therapist that her husband's behavior was socially and relationally unacceptable. She didn't get that and worse, never got to her deeper feelings of fear and anger. She fired the therapist after one session.

When we talked about this painful case, the therapist took the position of "let's be reasonable." He offered a laundry list of semi-hip observations about sexual liberation, comments on the wife's prudishness, sympathy for the husband's loneliness and absolutely no awareness of the reality that a fierce storm had assaulted the garden of their love and that no one and both of them were victims of it.

You might say the therapist himself was seduced and enchanted by his own courtroom orientation towards relationships. I later learned this therapist had been married and divorced several times himself, each time clinically dissecting his choice of partner. So add one more indication of the courtroom in your marriage – diagnoses, or analysis, or speculation, or evidence gathering, or theorizing. These are all strategies for avoiding relationships and have absolutely toxic effects when used as attempts to resolve relationship challenges.

B. Heroes and Heroines

To claim your song and transform your marriage will take great courage. Some of you spend a little time in the courtroom, some live there full time. Whatever your situation, transforming your relationship into a fecund, beautiful and elegant garden of delight that is capable of sustaining your enthusiasm for your marriage, will take consciousness of heroic proportions.

Healthy and Unhealthy Guilt

Guilt is represents the repression of anger, sorrow or deep frustration. Guilt is a thought, not really a feeling. A couple of generations of television watching have moved many of us away from taking full responsibility for our failure to love. Our loving continues to get shallower and shallower. We may blame our children for our inadequate loving of them or we may demand they perform and reassure us that we're okay. What we do is a reflection of our unwillingness to face the lifelessness in our own marriage.

Guilt comes in two forms – healthy and unhealthy. Healthy guilt is that thought/feeling I experience when, for example, I elect to work for luxuries instead of spending real time with my children. In a society where we trumpet "time is money," connecting the dots between how much attention I give to my need for toys versus how connected I am to the real needs of my children is an act of consciousness. The thought, when aware, is guilt, the feeling is anxiety. We handle this with tranquilizers. The thought is "this pursuit of toys to the detriment of quality parenting is immoral." We may handle the (unwelcome) thinking by distracting ourselves with entertainment and addictions. If you can welcome the healthy guilt that comes from truncating the health of your family you'll have leverage on yourself and, perhaps, the energy and courage to challenge your choices and change your path.

Unhealthy guilt is that kind of self-inflicted suffering that comes from anxiety over nothing more troubling than being fully who you are.

Unhealthy guilt says "I'm sorry" a lot. A person bathed in unhealthy guilt spends a lot of time in fear and can only live a small portion of life's promises.

Both kinds of guilt are uncomfortable. So if you want to be heroic in your marriage begin to look at real guilt – guilt that you experience as a result of living only a small part of the promise that brought you together. If you live in the courtroom and feel guilty because distance, coldness and denial deprive both of you, expose it your partner. You should examine your own neglect of the courage to love, of failing to take 100% responsibility for the quality of relationships within your marriage, of indulging self-righteousness, fear of intimacy or willingness to project your shortcomings on those around you.

On the other hand, you should confront the infantile part of you that feels guilty when you stand up for what you believe, for your authoritative loving, for your right to independence of choice, for your joy in living, for your curiosity and so on. This kind of guilt is learned and must be confronted so that you take away its power to control you.

What do heroes and heroines have to do with all this? Here's three examples of mythic characters who are seen as heroes or heroines in their stories. Let's start with Peter Pan.

a. Peter Pan is a children's story, or is it? Peter is a character I'd build a full day workshop for men around. He is relationally shallow, hangs out in a fantasy battle with a fantasy bad guy, his peer group of choice are "bad boys" and he continually frustrates and ignores his (feminine) conscience. Peter is an anti-hero, someone who rejects the obvious shallowness of contemporary culture's mundane restraints but who at the same time, doesn't capitalize on his courage to live outside the warmth of the hearth. Instead, he flies in and out of bedroom windows and continually circles as he looks down on reality. He might be a Wall Street banker, or an entertainer on a TV reality show (for more, take a look at Dan Kiley's *The Peter Pan Syndrome*.)

b. A character of stunning conscience and a contrast to Peter's endless flight of fancy is Psyche. Her story carries all the ingredients of a modern woman's (and man's) heroic drive to live her love fully. She is a good model because she embraces conflict, repeatedly faces her fear, believes in the reality of her own loving while working through the idealizing of her love, allows herself to emerge from adolescent naïveté and willingly takes on the work of loving as only an adult woman can.

Psyche's story begins in her own adolescence where, strangely, she is an oddball and outcast because of her great beauty and presence. Some worship her, and her fame soon begins to rival that of the goddess Aphrodite. Psyche's simple parents seek advice from a local seer and are told that the only thing to be done is to abandon her to the gods. In other words, kill her.

Chained to a tree high above the valley she is rescued by a kindly wind and carried down into a lush paradise far below. She discovers an unoccupied retreat/palace – it's not clear exactly what it is, but she's welcomed there and soon is living in lonely but sumptuous luxury. One night, a male guest who speaks words of love to her visits, and soon they are wildly in love. He returns night after night but he imposes one restriction on their loving – she may never, ever look upon his face. The story seems to know that men like loving beautiful women but aren't so keen on self-revelation.

Psyche's very ordinary sisters hear of her situation and respond with jealousy. The story offers a nice detail here letting us know of the sister's very ordinary marriages to old and fat kings. Psyche's story is as contemporary as a story can be. The marriages of the sisters are on the south side of what we call marginal marriages.

At any rate, the sisters journey to the distant land where Psyche lives and with their jealousy increasing by the moment, convince her to break her lover's rule. They tell her he must be a monster and convince her to look upon his face after he falls asleep. Psyche, in her naïveté and trust does that. But in doing so, she accidently spills a drop of hot oil from the lamp on him, and he awakens enraged by her breaking their agreement. Eros flies out the window and returns to his mother who, it just happens, is Aphrodite. Now look, this story has everything – a beautiful young woman who is still learning how to live in this world, a handsome young man who has not yet left his mother's abode, jealous women, even an incompetent and passive father. Psyche, though, has light in her and determination. Her heroism shows up in her journey into conscious loving. She faces the deep question of whether life is worth living. She faces obstacles on the way to facing Eros' mother. She faces incredible odds in meeting the four challenges on her way to self-realization. And, finally she faces death itself.

As my friend Malidoma Soma once said, consciousness in not a weekend at a retreat center.

   c. We have looked at Peter's eternal boyhood and we could all talk about the price many women pay for hooking up with an adolescent man. We have spent a few moments thinking about Psyche and her heroic drive to love fully and consciously. Now we'll visit a couple that gives us an abandoned daughter, a courageous prince, a witch who turns out to be an agent of freedom, and it all ends in the birth of a new generation of male and female consciousness. Interested?

The German word for lettuce is *rapunzel*. **Rapunzel's** parents lived on the very edge of a garden owned and maintained by a witch. We don't know her name but then, the dark world of witches is nameless. As the story begins, Rapunzel's mother is pregnant with her. One day she notices a bright green vegetable growing in the garden of the witch. She asks her husband to retrieve it. He declines. She insists. Finally he jumps the fence and brings the lettuce to her. This scene is repeated. The magical lettuce quickly grows back. His wife seems to have developed a serious craving for lettuce.

One day, as the hapless husband is bending over to pick the lettuce, the witch appears. Frightened, he tries to excuse himself for trespassing and stealing by blaming it on his wife. The witch surprisingly reassures him – "take all that you want." He is immensely relieved. As he leaves, she adds this: "…on one condition. When your baby is born you must bring her to me. I will raise her." He agrees.

I once told an audience of couples that of all fathers, the most dangerous had to be the passive father. We have no idea what he will do, and his fear is as likely to drive him to abandon his children (see the story of "Hansel and Gretel") as indulge them endlessly.

Rapunzel's father's passivity begins her story. Years later, living in a tower constructed by the witch, she meets her lover. The story gives us sweet details of their naïveté, innocence and determination to love. But we don't see much of Rapunzel's or her lover's heroism until they are forced out into the world where their faith in each other drives them to reconnect and begin their own lives, now with twins, a boy and a girl.

The most touching detail occurs when the blinded prince stumbles into a clearing driven there by the sound of Rapunzel's singing. Her tears upon seeing him again fall on his eyes and he can once again see. The sight of love.

C. Weddings and the Three Marriages Within

We are hard wired for a three-dimensional marriage – life in this world, life in our own inner world and life in our shared garden of delight. We live in this world, roommates for life, and we dream dreams of how life might be for us. We consciously, or not so consciously, dream a kingdom here on earth, our kingdom. It may be as small as a cabin in the woods or it may be as grandiose as a mansion on a hill. This kingdom contains the concretized dreams of the longing of our senses for beauty, space, rest and safety.

The achievement of this marriage – our personal kingdom established and prospering – is the natural consequence of the promises we strained toward on our wedding day.

If we move towards the realization of this first kingdom, other promises and dreams are pushing for birth as well. We long for a deep inner peace, an inner connection with mythic dimensions. Some call this an inner marriage. Seen this way it is a kind of healing of a profound split suffered, perhaps, at birth or soon after as we identified with our gender of destiny.

The marriage of masculine and feminine can also be experienced as a kind of new intimacy with our inner twin. This coming together, the experience of deep personal integration, is fundamental to loving. Without it, most days will be spent in distancing, diagnosing and loneliness. Another way of saying this is that Psyche knew two things – she had to achieve the integrity of her independence and, simultaneously, leave her independent way of loving. Her story, perhaps, invented the idea of healthy dependence in loving.

Notice that Peter's story leaves us wondering whether he ever will "get it." Whereas, Rapunzel knew she must leave the enchantment and control of the witch – a task which is hauntingly familiar to those who through psychotherapy and other means seek to transform their past history into meaningful living – to truly partner with her prince.

The third marriage then is the coming together in consciously chosen intimate connecting in love. This marriage is the one hidden in the promise of new love and is the foundation for our naming divorce as a promise aborted. Marriage, as realization of deep spiritual connecting, lifelong partnering and the "becoming one" of intimate connecting is what we know as the "third marriage" within marriage.

Popular culture – focused as it is on quick gratification of needs and a seductive offer for happiness in leaving agreements and choosing the latest new thing – tricks us and pull us away from what we once knew at the deepest levels of being. The stories' benefits may be to remind us of how we're built and what we really need.

We may then ask how do we use these insights to create a life together that honors our deepest needs, works with and through the distractions and seductions of modern life, and recognizes our choice of partner as a golden one.

D. Sustainable Enthusiasm in Marriage

I'll offer these in the form of a list so that you take what you need and leave the rest. Here are six critical ideas that you can dialogue about together. If you allow yourselves to enjoy the dialogue you will create your own marriage conversation and begin laying the foundations for sustainable enthusiasm in relationship.

1. Loving Anger

When I first started talking about this with couples, a man I have great respect for said this: "Loving anger? Isn't that a contradiction in terms?" I answered that in many of our histories our experience of anger was almost exclusively of a different sort. We experienced criticism, shaming and even violent anger. So it would not surprise me if in talking about anger, the first thing that would come to mind would be bad memories.

It may be, however, that every strong emotion we feel in relationship is connected to our loving. If that is so, it also may be true that the distortion of strong emotions is what is destructive, not the emotion itself.

I think of sorrow. Distorted it becomes self-pity. Sensuality can be distorted and look like entitlement. If we add a bit of addiction, sensuality can look like obsession. Joy mixed in with anxiety can look like hysteria. Anger, a healthy emotion, can distort into coldness or amp up into violence.

Loving anger takes anger seriously. Doesn't aim at someone else; instead, honors your own experience. If I'm angry you may have triggered it, but you can be pretty sure the anger I feel has a great deal more to do with me and my experience than with the triggering event.

A man walks into his living room after being gone several days on a very taxing business trip. The room is messy and obviously needs some tidying up. He mentions something to his teenage son and his son responds with "What's your problem? You've been home five minutes and all you do is complain." A serious shouting argument follows.

What to do? First, the anger the man felt probably had a lot more to do with the "untidiness" of several business conversations he had on the trip that didn't go well. Second, his standards for an orderly and comfortable home weren't part of the conversation. Loving anger might have looked – could have looked – like an invitation, "Hey, Bobby, give me a hand. Let's tidy this up." As he did so, he could be talking with his son about his frustrating trip, about his need to burn off some of the energy of that by cleaning up and about how much he missed being home. In doing so, he would be transforming his reactive anger into an invitation to collaborate with his son in an active expression of love.

Loving anger requires that you believe in your relationship, in the love that holds you together and in the good intentions of your partner. Opening up this discussion will give you lots of examples to brainstorm around. Doing that will increase your enthusiasm for continuity in relating.

2. Belief

It is an old but reliable truth: We get to create the world we live in. If we believe in our clichés we will see them come to pass – "the way women are," "men just don't get it," "all marriages sooner or later lose their glow," etc. Clichés come out of our history, from old and dead conversations and from the media. Some even may be true but in order to enjoy sustainable enthusiasm in marriage you'll have to challenge every cliché that comes up.

Once you begin to create a "cliché filter" you can begin to consciously create beliefs that are true for your marriage. For example, instead of saying to my men friends, "That's the way women are," I could say, "There's a great deal about my wife that's mysterious to me. She often says or does things I simply have no framework for understanding."

Beliefs aren't only about marquee issues. Most of our beliefs live below the radar of shared discussion. Work with exposing them – your own definition of marriage, what you think men need, what you think women need, your take on emotion in marriage, your ideas about spiritual vitality, your beliefs about physical connections and so on.

3. Forever? You bet

Caution: There are many Peter Pans out there and some of them are writing scripts for movies and sitcoms. Relationship transience may make people laugh but sitcoms generally will not show you much of the pain of fractured relationships or give much of a sense of how unsatisfying it can be.

Forever is, of course, an ideal because nothing is forever for humans. Commitment that lasts a lifetime offers huge benefits unmatched by any romantic notion of relationship musical chairs. There's pretty good evidence that lifetime commitment offers:

- healthier adults

- the opportunity to fully discover your own natural genius

- the opportunity to manifest the full possibilities of your loving

- economic advantage

- stronger communities

- greater possibilities for individuation

- safer and healthier children

So why do we continue to experience the burden of a + 50% divorce rate? We know that single parenting is close to a heroic challenge. We also know that children of single parent families are way over represented in drug and alcohol abuse, the criminal justice system and teenage pregnancies.

We offer that, in addition to many dysfunctional marriages happening on the run without any marriage education or real community support, there is also the core argument of this book: Many married unconsciously grounded in an old paradigm, "If we feel good, its gotta be right."

In order to take full advantage of "Forever? You bet," you'll have to consider creating a new working paradigm for marriage. We offer a starting point. You'll have to take what you can use and build your own model, one that's designed to make your marriage sing.

4. The Theater in Your Head

As soon as I invite a couple to create a new paradigm for the love they share, a paradigm that will inform how they show up in the world of marriage – questions come. "We're doing alright. I just want him to share more of himself with me. How will a new paradigm help that?" (attractive 30-something attorney and mother of two.)

She has a well-developed logician in her head. She likes things simple. A straight line is the shortest distance between two points kind of person. The idea of re-imagining the basis of their marriage doesn't excite her. So I say, "If I could show you multiple pathways to intimate conversation, would that interest you?" "Yes," she says. "Further, if I could show you a point of origin that, by repeatedly returning to it you could energize each of those pathways, would that interest you as well?" "Certainly," she says.

"And if I could show you that there are several basic needs hidden in each and every conversation and that recognition of those needs will dramatically increase the frequency of 'opening up,' would that get your attention?" "It would," she confessed.

What I have just offered you is the skeleton of a new paradigm for marriage, a model that will dramatically increase your partner's desire to "share" with you. Each of us has several "characters" living in our heads. We created them, often for purposes of survival. I have a "who cares" guy I created in my New Jersey childhood to shield myself from chronic disappointments. I know people who have a "I'm outta here" character, people who walk around with "poor me," or "I'm the queen" or "shut up and listen." Try naming a few of your own. These "characters" need to be identified so they don't run your life. Instead, *you* run your life and use the characters when helpful. And, by the way, introducing yourself to the characters in your head will give you an edge. Let me tell you how.

5. Living on the Edge

In relationships, it means you stay out of your comfort zone as much as possible. That doesn't mean you forgo comfort in this relationship. It means that you choose to stay away from the clichés that tempt you – that you do not indulge the "characters" in your head and give them freedom to dominate your behavior but instead keep a running dialogue going with them. If "who cares?" shows up for me I have to turn around and face him – as in "why do you want me to walk away from this encounter? What's in it for you?" In doing that I bring a barely conscious attitude into consciousness where I can hold it (and myself) accountable.

Living on the edge means that you admit to yourself that you know that you don't know all there is to know about your partner.

Living on the edge can look like genuine curiosity about who your honey is. It can look like taking a risk and telling them who you are, when who you are may not get applause. But even more than that, living on the edge means you're willing to ask new things from your marriage and that you aren't willing to settle for "hey honey I'm home. What's for dinner?"

A retired police officer and his legal secretary wife put it this way: "We once thought that the edge we wanted to live on was out there somewhere so we got involved with what some would say are extreme sports – bungee jumping, helicopter skiing, triathlons, that sort of thing. We soon noticed that our intimacy was stale. Wasn't growing.

We weren't growing. Hitch came home one night and said 'we gotta talk.'"

"After my initial uh oh! I started listening to him describe his coming retirement, his messing around with adult films after I went to sleep, his longing for something more." "The truth is," he said, "I want something more out of my life and I want it with you."

Hitch was 51. I reminded them of Carl Jung's observation about men. He said that up to roughly middle-age, men look at their lives from the point of view of their birth. "Gee, I'm 21, I can legally drink or vote or drive." Or, "I've been on this planet 25 years already and I don't yet have a career." Somewhere around middle-age, men begin to notice the obituaries. They begin to think of their father's age when he died, begin to notice the age of famous people when they die. Jung said that was a beginning of an appreciation for the meaning of one's own life. We begin to ask if we've ever really loved anyone, if our career is truly right for us, if we leave a legacy what will it be and even what kind of parent have I been.

I think those questions, if answered in a serious and straightforward way, are the difference between men becoming bitter old men, and men moving on into the next manifestation of meaning in their lives.

Edge would mean choosing your life in a way that is in harmony with your inner world. No applause here. Edge would mean asking real growth from your relationship instead of living in the old patterns and habits. Edge would mean experimenting with new ways of talking about your love, your lovemaking and your desires for this relationship as well as consciously giving up on all the ways that no longer nourish or interest you.

Living on the edge means you have to develop a capacity for change and growth.

6. Change? Oh, my!

It's going to happen. We can't stop it. Change is the only thing that doesn't change, the philosopher Heraclitus said. Change. "You look different today." Change. "I no longer like the color red." Change. "We've always made love on Saturday night." Change. "I just lost my job." Change. "We're going to have a grandchild." Change.

Healthy people embrace failure as opportunity and see change as inevitable. Healthy couples grow their competence in times of change. It is where they get a better look at their own loving, where they learn about how they are loved. Change is an opportunity to renew courage, strengthen dormant muscles and open new spiritual ground for exploration.

Wherever you are in your marriage, we invite you to invite change. Change your paradigm, discard some old beliefs, ask tough questions, challenge your own loving, take another look at conflict (if it's chronic, ask what are you doing; if it's absent, ask what are we missing) and create some new vows. Never, never, never, never give in to the illusion of arrival, of "That's all, folks," because it's never over until it is. And even that is a fact we're uncertain about.

X. The Promise

We've taken a long look (perhaps too long) at what's needed for you to embrace your marriage as it is today. We also promised a roadmap for taking your marriage from marginal to magnificent – a marriage that sings. Here's where we are.

When I recently enthusiastically gave my honey a piece I had just written on marriage she said this: "How can you write this when our marriage is so…ordinary?" "Well," I objected, "it isn't exactly ordinary. We have developed some competency in conflict, we mastermind vision (albeit in small pieces, lurching from conversation to conversation without neatness and order), we challenge each other and we like to hang out (that last offered rather limply)." She said, "Yes, we do, but you're telling people that their marriages can sing and we haven't really talked in days!"

The promise and the reality. I like my partner because my press releases don't distract her. We've been a work in progress for over 25 years and we both share a real sense that we're just beginning. I know I'm an idealist and I know that I want to cheerlead each of you into claiming a promise land that may look distant and for some unattainable. I believe we all can do it. I believe we can put the same kind of energy, conviction and passion into loving those we've chosen to love, grounding our commitments and thoughtfully working through our individual and partnership challenges that any successful enterprise would demand.

I believe that it's worth everything you will risk – your time, your pride, your 'safety zone,' your self-image, your various masks. I believe that claiming your right to live in a marriage that sings, lasts throughout your life, nourishes your children and your community is top priority. I believe that your life will be economically more successful, physically more healthful, spiritually more meaningful and emotionally more joyful if you invest yourself fully in claiming the promise of your love.

That's what I believe. I don't believe it's easy, I don't believe it happens on autopilot, I don't believe you'll hear oceans of applause for committing to this work, and I don't believe you will not doubt your capacity to make it happen.

But there are couples doing it. We know them. There are resources available. We'll show them to you. There is coaching, counseling, books, articles, podcasts, websites. You can get support through email coaching, phone coaching, individual and couple coaching. There are secular-based marriage education programs, religious-based marriage education programs and programs sponsored and paid for by government agencies. You are not alone in this. But, you need to commit. You need to be able to see through the challenges you face today and grab a line, a rope or a thread that will connect you to the energy and commitment of other couples all around the world who will not settle for ordinary. I'm not. And neither is my partner.

We offer our encouragement and support. Hugs all around.

APPENDIX
INDICATORS OF STRENGTHS AND WEAKNESSES
IN DOMAIN FUNCTIONING

Every individual will naturally be "stronger" in some areas (we see this as part of 'natural genius') and also more developed in some ways than in others. These indicators are meant to give you a sense of personal and relationship 'audit.' Use them as pathways for exploration and growth.

Domain One:
Roommates – The Outer Journey

Strong in Domain One:

- Life is appropriately orderly
- Good management of assets and resources
- Strong social relationships
- Community involvement: votes, P.T.A., service clubs
- Extended family connections are healthy and well managed
- Active in church or synagogue
- Children are appropriately responsible, active in community, have good friends, work well with challenges of school
- Leadership reflects ethical and moral values / is non hierarchal

- Cooperative and effective as roommates
- Exercise and eating habits are healthy
- Enjoys career and community
- Home is comfortable and clean, decorated appropriately to the values and style of those who live there
- Proactive problem solver
- Good at having fun, getting rest and recreation

Weak in Domain One:

- Home uncomfortable to be in
- Chronically argumentative
- Disarray, disordered, unclean home
- Manages affairs from crisis to crisis
- Air of impending doom / hysteria / anxiety characterizes home
- Leadership is power based
- Roommate interactions are guilt / power based
- Poor or non existent communication
- Unhappy in job, location of home, automobile, politics etc
- Politically inactive / cynical / reactionary – a 'prophet of doom'
- Few friends – feels unappreciated
- Extended family connections are dysfunctional
- Parents are managed
- Children are chronically and excessively needy
- Not active in community or active and demanding, controlling, self-absorbed

Domain Two:
Inner Work – The Inner Journey

Strong in Domain Two:

- A healthy sense of Self
- Conversant with your own dreams: remember them; record them; actively work with the images
- Personal history: aware of and encounters influences; separates self from motheand father's world; aware of own 'stepping stones'
- Spiritual life: aware of mortality, recognizes higher power; beliefs and values are clear; active in a spiritual community; quality of humility
- Gender: is clear about gender identity, articulate re: "inner partner," dream work utilized, inner work feeds Journey into Intimacy
- Sustainable enthusiasm for inner development
- Extended family awareness
- Ancestor wisdom a part of daily life
- Personal symbolism – clear, articulate and utilized in conscious relating
- Wounds and Losses: faced, grieved, integrated and used as resource
- Domains: know 'where' they are at all times

Weak in Domain Two:

- Low trust of partner / indulges projections
- Bickering
- Attracted to "taking a position"
- Analyze, diagnose, speculate, theorize, predict, dissect, critique, judge, scrutinize – their partners
- Distance problem: too much or too little / chronic struggle
- with boundaries
- Unhappy in career, life style, community…
- Vulnerable to addictions, affairs, obsessions
- Vulnerable to "quick fix" solutions / charismatic 'gurus'
- Moody / angry / sad / moods of frustration / restless / mood swings
- Reactive

Domain Three: The Journey into Intimacy

Strong in Domain Three: The Marriage of Body, Soul and Spirit

- Experiences the multi dimensional joy of intimacy often
- Knowledge of the sacred and inter-relationship with Eros
- Personally developed language for this domain
- Huge reverence for and honoring of "the intimate moment"
- Awareness of cyclical nature of the body's rhythms and relates this to challenges of intimacy

- Spiritual intimacy and emotional / psychgical / and physical intimacy consciously inter-related
- Works with developing intimate connections that open to deeper levels of awareness of partner
- Utilizes literature, poetry, song, and dance to enrich the "dance of intimacy"
- Evident humility
- Deep mutual respect
- Aware of the "third marriage"
- Creates 'sacred space' for connecting
- Creates 'sacred time' for connecting

Undeveloped in Domain Three:

- Makes no time for intimate conversation
- Makes no place for relationship exploration
- Passion is inaccessible
- Loss of spiritual and sensual vitality
- Inattentive to evolutionary possibilities of aging together
- Gender differences = a problem
- Avoids conflict by 'spiritualizing' / rationalizing / sexualizing or emotionalizing it. Conflict is power based
- No language skills or tools for this domain - person appears mute
- Weak in ability to 'conference' important decisions
- Stalled career
- Unaware of partner's personal challenges
- Physically bland or demanding
- Leadership is ineffective and / or impotent

The Author

STEPHEN W. FRUEH consults and coaches business leaders and corporate teams by assessing and impacting leadership effectiveness. He coaches couples on creating new approaches to "The Marriage Conversation," helping them to revitalize and renew their relationship.

These two dimensions of his work in many ways mirror each other: the leadership conversations contain personal factors that, when addressed, significantly expand an executive's impact and effectiveness; similarly, many couples are finding that carefully studying their personal paradigms opens a pathway to new energy, greater intimacy, clearer conversations, and increased relational competencies.

Stephen offers workshops with his wife Lynn – a marriage and family therapist – on a number of dimensions within the marriage conversation. They invite couples into a new way of thinking about marriage, one that sustains enthusiasm for the relationship and supports a life-long commitment.

Stephen is available as a keynote speaker. He is a member of the National Speakers Association and is an engaging workshop and seminar leader.

Stephen offers coaching and consulting services to businesses and couples who seek to more fully realize their potentials.

You can contact Stephen at **805 527 2600** (WTR) or **805 338 4286** or email him **Stephen@withtheserings.com**

TreeNeutral

Advantage Media Group is proud to be a part of the Tree Neutral™ program. Tree Neutral offsets the number of trees consumed in the production and printing of this book by taking proactive steps such as planting trees in direct proportion to the number of trees used to print books. To learn more about Tree Neutral, please visit **www.treeneutral. com.** To learn more about Advantage Media Group's commitment to being a responsible steward of the environment, please visit **www. advantagefamily.com/green**

From Marginal to Magnificent is available in bulk quantities at special discounts for corporate, institutional, and educational purposes. To learn more about the special programs Advantage Media Group offers, please visit **www.KaizenUniversity.com** or call 1.866.775.1696.

Advantage Media Group is a leading publisher of business, motivation, and self-help authors. Do you have a manuscript or book idea that you would like to have considered for publication? Please visit **www.amgbook.com**